MW01110430

RETHINKING THE ENTERPRISE

Insights from the world's leading CEOs

Saul Berman, Peter Korsten and Ragna Bell
Foreword by Michael Tushman

Rethinking the Enterprise

Rethinking the Enterprise
Published by Gti Media
Level 6, 69 Reservoir Street
Surry Hills, Sydney
NSW 2010 Australia
info@gtimedia.com.au

Publisher: Ashley Russell
Editor-in-chief: Hugh Lamberton
Design: Gti Studios

First edition published January 2010.
ISBN 978-0-646-52494-8
© IBM Corporation 2010.

All paper used in the production of this publication is sourced
from sustainable forests.

RETHINKING THE ENTERPRISE

Insights from the world's leading CEOs

Saul Berman, Peter Korsten and Ragna Bell

Foreword by Michael Tushman

Contents

Foreword

Michael Tushman

IBM's third biennial Global CEO Study found that business and public sector leaders were expecting unprecedented change within their environment. However, few anticipated the degree of financial and economic turmoil in the second half of 2008, which has tested organizations' ability to adapt to a new economic environment. We have seen some of the largest and most prominent organizations – such as General Motors in the automotive industry and Lehman Brothers in banking – file for bankruptcy. But we have also seen companies take advantage of the disruptions in their market.

This leads to an interesting question: Why is it that some large, successful organizations fail, but others survive and thrive? Luck has to be part of it, but so do effective management and the firm's ability to adapt. Drawing on Darwin's evolutionary thinking, we know that neither strength nor intelligence alone guarantees survival. Only the ability to adapt can do that.

In our most recent research, Charles O'Reilly and I explore the topic of organizational adaptability in the context of recent advances in evolutionary theory. We found that in the face of significant technological and market change – as we are now experiencing – successful organizations are able to effectively manage the process of selection within their own organization. Organizational *ambidexterity*, or the dynamic capability of an organization to simultaneously explore and exploit, accounts for this ability to adapt. Long-lived organizations continue to morph by adding new groups and new businesses while at the same time discontinuing or divesting lower-growth, low-margin businesses.

This requires a deliberate approach that uses existing firm assets and capabilities and reconfigures them to address new opportunities. When done explicitly, this involves targeted investments and promotes organizational learning. It embodies a complex set of cultures and routines, including decentralization, differentiation and targeted integration. The senior team's ability to articulate and support paradoxical strategies – strategies for today and tomorrow – is a crucial determinant of these dynamic capabilities. So, too, is the senior team's ability to orchestrate the complex trade-offs that ambidexterity requires.

As organizations build the capabilities needed for long-term survival, they must explore and choose opportunities for the future while simultaneously exploiting their existing business. In the papers that follow, the IBM Strategy and Change leadership team provides a vision of the Enterprise of the Future that focuses on the challenge of performing today while simultaneously transforming for tomorrow. The Enterprise of the Future enables its strategy by driving continuous adaptation and change as it innovates with customers and redefines its business mix, operating model and culture to build sustainability into its future. The new economic environment has raised the stakes for those who fail to build adaptation explicitly into each enterprise's management system. The shaping of these dynamic capabilities is a crucial job of the leader and his or her team.

Michael Tushman
Paul R. Lawrence MBA Class of 1942 Professor of Business Administration, Harvard Business School.

Rethinking the enterprise

An introduction

Saul Berman, Peter Korsten and Ragna Bell

The disruptions spurred by the global financial crisis of 2008-09 have created an increasingly complex and uncertain economic environment. Faced with an accelerated rate of change, organizations are now rethinking their strategy and business models – what value they deliver, where to compete, how to take advantage and how to position for leadership in this new environment. This book draws on the findings of a substantial two-year research effort on precisely these issues and provides guidance on how organizations can position for sustainable success in the future.

We begin with the findings of IBM's third biennial Global CEO Study, based on in-depth conversations with more than 1,000 CEOs, senior business executives and public sector leaders, drawn from organizations of all sizes across a diverse range of industries and geographies. By combining these candid discussions of experiences, plans and aspirations with detailed theoretical and statistical analyses, we have developed a unique understanding of what we call the Enterprise of the Future.

The subsequent six chapters delve more deeply into the tremendous challenges posed by the new economic environment and the key traits required by organizations to survive and succeed. Our continued research provides strategic and tactical insights based on the differences in strategy and performance between companies that have failed or underachieved and those swift and agile enterprises that do not merely cope with change but turn it to their advantage.

To further explore the themes raised in each chapter, we include perspectives from leading business executives, who draw on their experiences at companies including IKEA, Publicis Groupe, Tata Motors, Verizon, Li & Fung, Bharti Airtel and Coca-Cola.

What will the Enterprise of the Future look like? **Chapter 1 (The Enterprise of the Future: The 2008 Global CEO Study)** provides an answer to this question based on insights from CEOs from around the world. They told us that:

- Organizations are bombarded by change, and many are struggling to keep up
- CEOs view their more demanding customers not as a threat, but as an opportunity to differentiate
- Nearly all CEOs are adapting their business models and two thirds are implementing extensive business model innovations
- CEOs are moving aggressively toward global business designs
- Financial outperformers anticipate more change, manage it better and engage in bolder plays

By closely examining the common themes in their comments we have been able to isolate the essential elements of the successful Enterprise of the Future. It is:

- Hungry for change
- Innovative beyond customer imagination
- Globally integrated
- Disruptive by nature
- Genuine, not just generous

When we talked to CEOs for the 2008 CEO Study, they were clearly prepared for substantial change, and were in fact optimistic about that. But few, if any, anticipated the severity of the financial and economic turmoil to come – a new environment in which many companies have found themselves fighting for survival, with extreme constraints on access to credit and capital, falling demand and increased price sensitivity among customers, and disruption of supply chains, partnerships and customer arrangements. New regulatory regimes are adding to the complexity of the challenge.

Indeed, one of the most valuable features of the research program that underpins this book has been the opportunity to observe and learn from the impact of the global financial and economic crisis. Our analysis of early winners from the crisis and of historical data points to three broad strategies: focus on value; exploit opportunities; and act with speed. In **Chapter 2 (Succeeding in the new economic environment: Focus on value, opportunity, speed)**, we outline the actions necessary to implement these strategies successfully and set the stage for leadership in the new economic environment.

The remaining chapters drill deeper into the five essential elements of the Enterprise of the Future. They incorporate fresh data and survey results to explore their relevance and application in the context of the new economic environment.

While the Enterprise of the Future is "hungry for change," successful execution remains the exception. Yet the rewards can be great. Analysis shows that the best performers often use times of turbulence to increase competitive advantage. New research on "change masters" provides strong evidence that fundamental strategies for successful change do exist and can be applied in good times and bad. **Chapter 3 (Making change work: Closing the change gap)** shows that project success most often depends on people-related issues. Based on data from IBM's Making Change Work study, the chapter identifies four factors – the elements of what we call the "change diamond" – that can help practitioners lead successful change by addressing their greatest project challenges.

The Enterprise of the Future is "innovative beyond customer imagination," surpassing the expectations of increasingly demanding customers. This capability is being deeply tested in the new economic environment, and is now more important than ever before. Consumer behavior has fundamentally changed, the world is increasingly digital and the viability of existing business models is being challenged. **Chapter 4 (The path forward: New models for customer-focused leadership)** urges customer relationship management and marketing professionals to quickly focus on developing the customer insight and digital-channel leadership that will allow them to transform customer experience, open new markets and reduce organizational complexity.

Global integration, too, has become more important. It supports growth strategies, improves operational performance, increases flexibility and access to capital and resources and delivers cost savings. Yet business leaders often stumble when establishing the operational capabilities needed to support global integration. **Chapter 5 (The R-O-I of globally integrated operations: Strategies for enabling global integration)** delivers a practical framework that can be employed to achieve this. Based on our experience and an analysis of 20 diverse best-practice examples, the "R-O-I framework" emphasizes repeatable processes, optimized assets and integrated operations, all on a global basis and supported by strong leadership, organizational structures and technology.

Business model innovation is critical to success – and business leaders know it as they become "disruptive by nature." Indeed, 98 percent of the companies surveyed by IBM reported pursuing business model innovation to some extent. Based on follow-up of *The Enterprise of the Future* and an analysis of 28 successful business model innovators, **Chapter 6 (Seizing the advantage: When and how to innovate your business model)** argues that organizations can determine the right timing based on the economic environment, the degree of transformation in their industry and a set of internal factors, such as the deployment of new products or services. To improve execution, business model innovators must pay heed to what we call the Three A's: Organizations must be *aligned* with customer value; *analytical* to gain insight from differentiated intelligence; and enabled by an *adaptable* operating model.

And finally, in **Chapter 7 (Leading a sustainable enterprise: Leveraging insight and information to act)**, we focus on the need for organizations to be "genuine, not just generous." Surprisingly perhaps, given the economic challenges, 60 percent of global business leaders surveyed by IBM in early 2009 said corporate social responsibility (CSR) had become more important to them over the past year, a period that included the worst of the financial crisis. Why are they focused on it? Business leaders see CSR as a way to achieve both cost efficiency and growth opportunities – in a more sustainable way. There is no doubt organizations have sharpened their focus on sustainability, primarily in response to consumer and stakeholder expectations. However, most lack the information they need. Based on the experiences of outperforming organizations and CSR leaders, we argue that businesses must develop new sources of operational, supply chain and customer information to gain the insights needed to meet strategic sustainability objectives.

And so, grounded in the collective wisdom of our interviewees and our ongoing research program, we offer *The Enterprise of the Future* and the follow-on studies to CEOs, corporate officers and boards of directors around the world as a benchmark, blueprint and catalyst for further discussion. It is an aspirational goal. Some companies already exhibit particular traits, but few, if any, possess them all. Based on our conversations and analyses, we believe that significant financial opportunity awaits those that become Enterprises of the Future.

* * *

We would like to offer our gratitude to all of the private and public sector leaders who so generously shared their time and ideas and to the many colleagues who have contributed their insight and guidance. Their thoughts have played an invaluable role in defining the Enterprise of the Future and in our subsequent research. For that we are extremely grateful.

ABOUT THE EDITORS

Saul Berman is a Partner and Global Executive of IBM Global Business Services and leads the IBM Global Strategy and Change consulting practice. He has more than 25 years' experience consulting with senior management, focusing on competitive positioning, new business plans and strategies, new business models, growth and operational and cost improvement. His clients include most of the major media companies, as well as telecommunications and retail companies. He has published extensively and is a frequent keynote speaker at major conferences. He was named one of the 25 most influential consultants of 2005 by *Consulting* magazine. He can be contacted at saul.berman@us.ibm.com.

Peter Korsten is a Partner and Global Executive in IBM Global Business Services and is the Global Leader for the IBM Institute for Business Value. He is the Executive Director of the Global CEO Study, and led the development of *The Enterprise of the Future*. He has more than 20 years' experience advising an array of Fortune 500 companies on corporate and business strategy, including leading consumer products and industrial firms across Europe. He regularly speaks at external conferences on corporate strategy and leadership. He was named one of the 25 most influential consultants of 2008 by *Consulting* magazine. He can be contacted at peter.korsten@nl.ibm.com.

Ragna Bell is the Global Strategy and Change lead for the IBM Institute for Business Value within IBM Global Business Services. She has more than ten years of consulting experience with leading clients, focusing on mergers and acquisitions, customer segmentation, market analysis and corporate transformation. She has co-authored articles on business model innovation and is the Global Program Director for IBM's 2010 Global CEO Study. She can be reached at ragna.bell@us.ibm.com.

The Enterprise of the Future

Insights from more than 1,000 CEOs worldwide

To understand what the successful Enterprise of the Future will look like, IBM conducted in-depth interviews with more than 1,000 CEOs, general managers and senior public sector leaders from around the world. These conversations, together with our statistical and financial analyses, provide a unique perspective on the future of business and the key traits required to thrive in the new economic environment. Their collective wisdom points to an enterprise that is: hungry for change; innovative beyond customer imagination; globally integrated; disruptive by nature; and genuine, not just generous.

The Enterprise of the Future is the third edition of IBM's biennial Global CEO Study series. This research is based on interviews with more than 1,000 CEOs, general managers and senior public sector and business leaders drawn from 40 nations and 32 industries, from emerging and established economies.[1] Nineteen percent were from companies employing more than 50,000 employees while 22 percent had fewer than 1,000 employees.

As part of our research, we sought to understand differences between the responses of financial outperformers and those of underperformers. For companies with publicly available financial information, we compared revenue and profit track records with the averages for those in the same industry across our sample.[2] Companies that performed above average on a particular financial benchmark were tagged as outperformers and those below the average as underperformers. Throughout our analyses, we looked for insights based on these top- and bottom-half groupings.

FIGURE 1 **MORE THAN 1,000 CEOS WORLDWIDE PARTICIPATED IN THIS STUDY**
Our sample was geographically diverse and spanned both emerging and established economies.

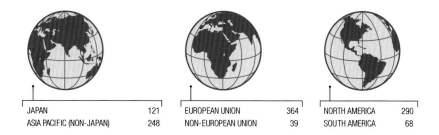

| JAPAN | 121 | EUROPEAN UNION | 364 | NORTH AMERICA | 290 |
| ASIA PACIFIC (NON-JAPAN) | 248 | NON-EUROPEAN UNION | 39 | SOUTH AMERICA | 68 |

CEOs are rapidly positioning their businesses to capture the growth opportunities they see. Our discussions about their plans and challenges revealed several striking findings:

- **Organizations are bombarded by change, and many are struggling to keep up.** Eight out of ten CEOs see significant change ahead, and yet the gap between expected change and the ability to manage it has almost tripled since the 2006 Global CEO Study.
- **CEOs view more demanding customers not as a threat, but as an opportunity to differentiate.** CEOs are spending more to attract and retain increasingly prosperous, informed and socially aware customers.
- **Nearly all CEOs are adapting their business models – two thirds are implementing extensive innovations.** More than 40 percent are changing their enterprise models to be more collaborative.
- **CEOs are moving aggressively toward global business designs, deeply changing capabilities and partnering more extensively.** CEOs have moved beyond the cliché of globalization, and organizations of all sizes are reconfiguring to take advantage of global integration opportunities.
- **Financial outperformers are making bolder plays.** These companies anticipate more change, and manage it better. They are also more global in their business designs, partner more extensively and choose more disruptive forms of business model innovation.

These findings – across industries, geographies and organizations of different sizes – paint a surprisingly similar view of the traits that we believe will be needed for future success. At its core, the Enterprise of the Future is ...

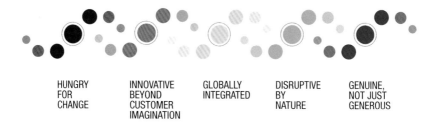

HUNGRY FOR CHANGE	INNOVATIVE BEYOND CUSTOMER IMAGINATION	GLOBALLY INTEGRATED	DISRUPTIVE BY NATURE	GENUINE, NOT JUST GENEROUS

- **Hungry for change.** The Enterprise of the Future is capable of changing quickly and successfully. Instead of merely responding to trends, it shapes and leads them. Market and industry shifts are a chance to move ahead of the competition.
- **Innovative beyond customer imagination.** The Enterprise of the Future surpasses the expectations of increasingly demanding customers. Deep collaborative relationships allow it to surprise customers with innovations that make both its customers and its own business more successful.
- **Globally integrated.** The Enterprise of the Future is integrating to take advantage of today's global economy. Its business is strategically designed to access the best capabilities, knowledge and assets from wherever they reside in the world and apply them wherever required in the world.
- **Disruptive by nature.** The Enterprise of the Future radically challenges its business model, disrupting the basis of competition. It shifts the value proposition, overturns traditional delivery approaches and, as soon as opportunities arise, reinvents itself and its entire industry.
- **Genuine, not just generous.** The Enterprise of the Future goes beyond philanthropy and compliance and reflects genuine concern for society in all actions and decisions.

This chapter presents findings related to each of these attributes of the Enterprise of the Future. It draws on the rich insights from our CEOs through statistical and financial analyses as well as the voices of the CEOs themselves. Each section concludes with some implications and thoughts about how organizations can move toward becoming an Enterprise of the Future and a case study to illustrate a leading company. These main attributes will be examined more deeply in later chapters of this book.

Hungry for change

CEOs foresee significant change ahead. But their confidence in their ability to manage that change is not nearly as high. So how will CEOs fare in an increasingly frenetic environment? Will they be able to respond effectively?

The change gap triples

In the 2006 IBM Global CEO Study, we were surprised when two thirds of the CEOs said their organizations were facing "substantial" or "very substantial" change over the next three years. But in 2008, even more CEOs – eight out of ten – expect such change.

This rising change challenge may be difficult for companies to meet. CEOs rate their ability to manage change 22 percentage points lower than their expected need for it – a "change gap" that has nearly tripled since 2006. While the number of companies successfully managing change has increased slightly, the number reporting limited or no success has risen by 60 percent.

FIGURE 2 **THE CHANGE GAP**
As the level of expected change continues to rise, many CEOs are struggling to keep up.

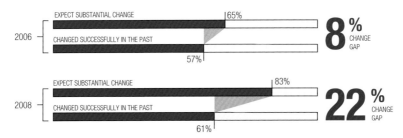

Faster, broader, more uncertain change

So what's causing this growing gap? Constant change is certainly not new. But companies are struggling with its accelerating pace. Everything around them seems to be changing faster than they can. As one US CEO told us, "We are successful, but slow."

> "We have seen more change in the last ten years than in the previous 90."
>
> *Ad J. Scheepbouwer, CEO, KPN Telecom*

CEOs are also wrestling with a broader set of challenges, which introduces even greater risk and uncertainty. In 2004, market factors, such as customer trends, market shifts and competitors' actions, dominated the CEO agenda. Other external factors – socioeconomic, geopolitical and environmental issues – were seen as less critical, and rarely made it to the CEO's desk.

But in 2008, CEOs are no longer focused on a narrow priority list. People skills are now just as much in focus as market factors, and environmental issues demand twice as much attention as they did in the past. Suddenly everything is important. And change can come from anywhere. CEOs find themselves – as one chief executive from Canada put it – in a "white-water world."

CEOs are most concerned about the impact of three external forces: market factors; people skills; and technology (see Figure 3). Customer expectation shifts, competitive threats and industry consolidation continue to weigh on their minds. CEOs are also searching for industry, technical and particularly management skills to support geographic expansion and replace aging baby boomers who are exiting the workforce. They rated insufficient talent as the top barrier to global integration – even higher than regulatory and budgetary hurdles. CEOs also described how technological advances are reshaping value chains, influencing products and services and changing how their companies interact with customers.

FIGURE 3 **TOP THREE CHANGE DRIVERS**
CEOs rated market factors, people skills and technological factors as the
three external forces with the greatest impact on their organizations.[3]

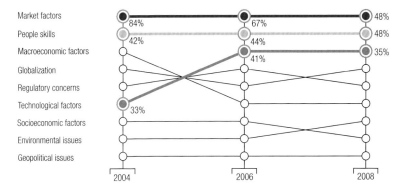

(Market factors) "The market is so dynamic. Visibility is very low."
Electronics CEO

(People skills) "We're making acquisitions for the people, not the assets."
Financial markets CEO

(Technology) "Technology is driving huge changes in our industry
landscape." Government health agency leader

FIGURE 4 **GAP IS SMALLER FOR OUTPERFORMERS**
Because outperformers manage change well, they can get ahead
of – and even be the drivers of – change.

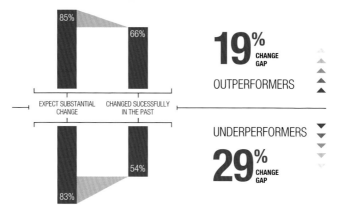

When we looked at the financial outperformers in our sample, it was apparent that their change gap was much smaller than that of underperformers.[4] The smaller change gap is not because they face fewer challenges or expect less change. Outperformers actually anticipate more change. Outperformers are simply more successful at managing change.

IMPLICATIONS

Clearly, the ability to change quickly and successfully is becoming more critical than ever before. Here are a few thoughts about how the Enterprise of the Future approaches change:

Accepts change as a state of being. The Enterprise of the Future sees change within the organization as a permanent state. Because of the company's culture, employees are comfortable with unpredictability. In an environment in which products, markets, operations and business models are always in flux, values and goals provide alignment and cohesion.

Hires, positions and rewards innovators and change leaders. The Enterprise of the Future is home to visionary challengers – people who question assumptions and suggest radical, and what some might initially consider impractical, alternatives. It also strategically places charismatic leaders who set direction, inspire and move the organization forward. High performers earn differentiated rewards, such as a stake in the business they helped create.

Focuses on delivering business outcomes. In a 2008 study of change management practices, 75 percent of the companies surveyed said their approach to change management was usually informal, ad hoc or improvised.[5]

In contrast, the Enterprise of the Future defines and manages change as robust programs, structured around and driven to deliver defined business outcomes. It tracks the business benefits of change and change management effectiveness. Strong change management is a core competence at all levels and nurtured as a professional discipline, not an "art."

Operates like a venture capitalist. The Enterprise of the Future establishes processes and structures that promote innovation and transformation. It manages a portfolio of investments, protecting and supporting the fledgling ideas, while systematically weeding out the weak ones.

ARE YOU READY?

- Does your organization have a healthy appetite for change?

- Have you seeded your organization with visionary challengers and provided them with the freedom to effect meaningful change?

- Do you manage change as a structured program and measure change management effectiveness?

- Do you have robust processes in place to incubate new product, service and business model concepts – and redirect investment when required?

CASE STUDY
ABB: Engineering enterprise-wide change

Switzerland-based automation firm ABB launched its Step Change Program in 2003 to improve productivity and cut costs. Hundreds of measures were identified and executed on schedule, resulting in annual savings of more than $US900 million. Launched in 2005 and still under way, the One Simple ABB Program is reducing organizational complexity and establishing common, global processes for finance, human resources and information services.

The impetus for these programs was a decision in late 2002 to focus on the company's core expertise in power and automation. This meant selling non-core businesses – such as upstream oil, gas and petrochemicals units – and outsourcing non-differentiating functions.

ABB's change programs today consist of a broad portfolio of initiatives with specific business and financial objectives. With members representing five global divisions, group functions and geographic markets, the ABB executive committee tracks progress and provides regional accountability. With its proven change-management capabilities, ABB is well positioned for the future – an organization engineered for change.

The results? ABB's successful focus on its strengths as a global leader in power and automation technology, and its improved productivity and cost structure, were driven largely by these enterprise-wide change programs. In 2007, ABB's net income increased to a record $US3.8 billion.[6]

Innovative beyond customer imagination

CEOs are investing heavily to capture rising prosperity opportunities worldwide. They are also investing more to serve increasingly sophisticated and demanding customers. But what will it take to convert these investments into greater market share?

Heavy investment in new markets

In rapidly developing economies worldwide, the middle class is growing and becoming progressively more prosperous. Greater disposable income brings new demand for more sophisticated, higher-value products and services. As one real estate CEO from India highlights, "In India, 400 million consumers will demand new housing in the next 20 years – that's more real estate than the United States has built since the Second World War."

Meanwhile, in established economies, significant wealth accumulation among aging baby boomers and a corresponding increase in young, affluent inheritors are boosting prosperity in what some might otherwise consider flat-growth markets.

In both developed and rapidly developing economies, rising prosperity is creating growth opportunities for many companies – and CEOs are upbeat about this trend. However, CEOs cautioned that using the same go-to-market strategies, products and services seldom works. Tapping into these new geographic and demographic segments will require a deeper understanding of these customers and a more tailored approach.

FIGURE 5 **TWO THIRDS OF CEOS SEE OPPORTUNITY AND ARE INVESTING**
CEOs will devote more than one quarter of their total annual investments to capture rising prosperity opportunities.[7]

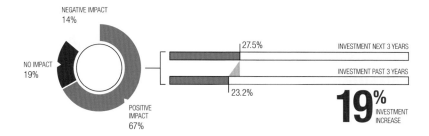

NEGATIVE IMPACT
14%

NO IMPACT
19%

POSITIVE
IMPACT
67%

27.5% INVESTMENT NEXT 3 YEARS

INVESTMENT PAST 3 YEARS

23.2%

19% INVESTMENT
INCREASE

Informed and collaborative customers: a chance to differentiate

In addition to the diverse needs of new markets, CEOs face rising expectations from increasingly informed and collaborative customers.

Customers now have far more sources of information, and the enterprise is no longer the definitive authority. In a recent survey of 1,000 retail consumers, 53 percent said they used the Internet to compare product features and prices – 25 percent did so from a mobile device while in a store. And one in ten sent text messages to friends and family during shopping trips to get input or share information on products.[8]

With the billion-user Internet, customers can broadcast expectations and share views worldwide – and publicly grade a company's performance against those indicators. Like-minded customers can network socially and pool their influence. And in an increasing number of industries, customers are swapping passive roles for much deeper involvement. "Consumers" are becoming "producers," creating entertainment and advertising content for their peers and even generating their own electricity.

> "In the future, we will be talking more and more about the 'prosumer' – a consumer/producer who is even more extensively integrated into the value chain. As a consequence, production processes will be customized more precisely and individually."
>
> *Hartmut Jenner, CEO, Alfred Kärcher GmbH*

This informed and collaborative customer "can be both a threat and an opportunity," as one media CEO from Belgium pointed out. Despite the potential downside, CEOs are on the whole optimistic.

FIGURE 6 **CEOS ARE UPBEAT ABOUT INFORMED AND COLLABORATIVE CUSTOMERS**
CEOs are focused on the opportunity, not the threat – and are investing accordingly.[9]

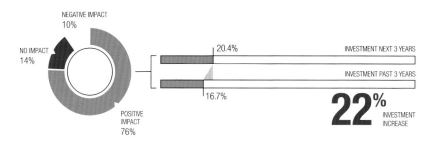

NEGATIVE IMPACT 10%
NO IMPACT 14%
POSITIVE IMPACT 76%

INVESTMENT NEXT 3 YEARS 20.4%
INVESTMENT PAST 3 YEARS 16.7%

22% INVESTMENT INCREASE

Many CEOs consider serving the informed and collaborative customer as an opportunity to distinguish their organizations – a chance to justify premium positioning and price. "The more informed our customers are and the higher their expectation levels, the better we will be positioned to demonstrate our differentiation," one US CEO told us.

Outperformers investing more

Financial outperformers are devoting more than 30 percent of their total annual investments to capture opportunities from rising prosperity worldwide.[10] Over the next three years, these new market investments will increase – but not as quickly as those targeting informed and collaborative customers. Outperformers plan to spend 36 percent more to serve these increasingly sophisticated customers.[11]

FIGURE 7 **OUTPERFORMERS ARE INCREASING THEIR CUSTOMER-RELATED INVESTMENTS**
Outperformers are already investing heavily in rising prosperity worldwide, and are rapidly increasing their investment in informed and collaborative customers.

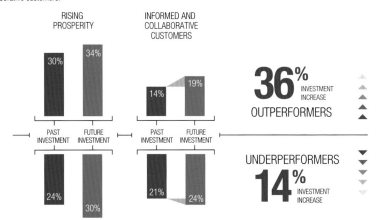

IMPLICATIONS

The Enterprise of the Future aims beyond articulated needs and wants, creating first-of-a-kind products, services and experiences that were never asked for – but are precisely what customers desire. Here are some thoughts about how it accomplishes this:

Finds ways to make offerings relevant to new markets and increasingly prosperous consumers. Global brands, products and services deliver economies of scale, yet each market has its own culture, needs and aspirations. The Enterprise of the Future constantly experiments and learns how to optimize the balance. It analyzes potential markets to find niches, white space and complacent competitors that allow it to capitalize on its core strengths.

Understands timing and network effects. There is a fine line between "beyond" and "too far." The Enterprise of the Future understands the need to introduce innovation that the market is ready to accept and works to perfect its market-entry timing. It exploits the network effects of early adoption to take a commanding early lead.

Connects everyone to the customer. Employees at all levels – from designers to warehouse employees – connect with customers through real-time information, online interaction or, where possible, in person. The Enterprise of the Future also develops deep relationships with leading-edge customers and employees – those early adopters who determine market success or failure. It test-markets in these communities and collaborates with them to develop products. In the business-to-business space, the Enterprise of the Future invests to integrate its systems with those of its key customers. This allows it to be a more active partner and an integral part of its customers' businesses.

Uses technology to anticipate shifts faster than the competition. Market insights are critical to the Enterprise of the Future. It recognizes the value of the information it collects through its many channels and mines the data for insights. It uses emerging technologies, such as virtual worlds, to gain insights in new ways. It also puts in place systems that allow very fast feedback cycles. When customer preferences and demand start to shift, it knows before the competition.

ARE YOU READY?

- Which of your offerings are breaking new ground, opening entirely new segments or markets? What can you learn from them?

- Are you systematically evaluating potential geographic markets? How do you achieve the efficiencies of global brands, products and services while remaining locally relevant?

- When customer preferences shift, are you the first to understand and act on this or do your competitors react more quickly?

- Are you effectively integrating disparate data and systems to gain new customer insights?

CASE STUDY
NINTENDO: BUILDING MARKET SHARE THROUGH
CUSTOMER COLLABORATION

In the early 1990s, Nintendo's share of the game console market was 61 percent, but by the mid-2000s, it had fallen to 22 percent.[12] To regain its leadership position, Nintendo needed to find new ways to delight gamers – and to bring gaming to new audiences.

To do that, Nintendo went straight to the source – gamers themselves. The company established an online community by offering incentives in return for customer information. The company also selected a group of experienced gamers based on the value and frequency of their community contributions. These "Sages" were given exclusive rewards, such as previews of new games, in exchange for helping new users and providing community support.[13]

Through this community, Nintendo has gained valuable insights into market needs and preferences. This has influenced everything from game offerings – such as an online library of "nostalgic" games that appeal to older gamers – to new product design – for example, the intuitive controls of the popular Nintendo Wii system, which have helped attract new, casual gamers.[14]

By leveraging the loyalty and expertise of its core customer segment, Nintendo has successfully connected with two new ones – women and older men. This collaboration seems to have paid off: Nintendo is once again ahead of its competitors, with 44 percent market share.[15]

Globally integrated

CEOs face many choices when responding to global integration. How should they design their businesses to take advantage of capabilities located in other parts of the world? When should they partner, merge or acquire? Which markets should they enter? In all this complexity, which strategies work best?

Radical changes in business design to capitalize on global integration

As the world becomes more connected and more accessible, CEOs see tremendous opportunities to expand their global reach, tapping into new sources of expertise and new markets. Traditional views of globalization – labor arbitrage and riding the wave of economic growth in China and India – are being replaced by a new focus: global integration. By this, they mean new business designs that facilitate faster and more extensive collaboration on a worldwide scale and rapid reconfiguration when new opportunities appear. In our interviews, we explored how CEOs are recalibrating their business designs to take advantage of increasing global integration. Their responses are outlined in Figure 8.

CEOs often had ready answers for this series of potentially complex questions and options. Clearly, they had been thinking through these issues for some time because they are critical levers to exploit the opportunities of global integration. It was striking that CEOs of companies of all different sizes and geographic coverage were engaged and enthusiastic about these topics, which suggests optimization is crucial whatever the current geographic scale.

FIGURE 8 **CEOS ARE EMBARKING ON MAJOR CHANGES TO THEIR BUSINESS DESIGNS**
We asked CEOs to score their global integration plans along seven continuums.
Most of their answers lean toward more global optimization.

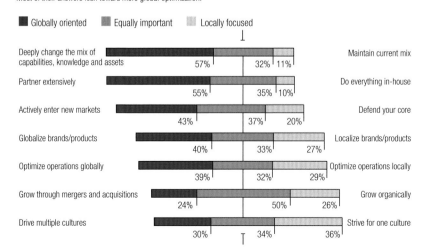

■ Globally oriented ▨ Equally important ▨ Locally focused

	Globally oriented	Equally important	Locally focused	
Deeply change the mix of capabilities, knowledge and assets	57%	32%	11%	Maintain current mix
Partner extensively	55%	35%	10%	Do everything in-house
Actively enter new markets	43%	37%	20%	Defend your core
Globalize brands/products	40%	33%	27%	Localize brands/products
Optimize operations globally	39%	32%	29%	Optimize operations locally
Grow through mergers and acquisitions	24%	50%	26%	Grow organically
Drive multiple cultures	30%	34%	36%	Strive for one culture

Deep changes in capability and asset mix

Across the entire CEO sample, more than half plan to deeply change their organizations' capabilities, knowledge and assets. New customer expectations are driving some of these shifts. "We need to move away from an operational focus to a client interface focus," one US CEO said. "This requires new skills and a new skill mix for the corporation."

Operating in new geographies was another reason for updating the mix. "We made the same mistake as everyone else – simply using our existing domestic team to drive our international business," explained the CEO of an Asian utility company. "Then we realized this does not work. We have now built a team with the right mix of business and capital development skills."

Though CEOs had various reasons for changing the mix, they agreed on one point: It is difficult to do. One French CEO saw this as his "most important shift," but also "the space with the most change and difficulties."

> "A few years ago, we were a national company; now we're a global company. Our integrated supply chain must adapt to meet demand in 50 countries. We're going to have to bring people in from the outside."
>
> *Jim Guyette, President and CEO, Rolls-Royce North America*

Partnering is pervasive – especially among outperformers

Eighty-five percent of CEOs plan to partner to capitalize on global integration opportunities – more than half plan to do so extensively. We also found that outperformers are 20 percent more likely to partner extensively than underperformers.[16] This reinforces what we discovered in the previous Global CEO Study – extensive collaborators outperform their competitive peers.[17] CEOs see partners as a source of valuable talent – an ingredient in short supply. "Partnering has shifted from tactical 'Enter a new market' to strategic 'Access to capabilities'," explained one CEO from Hong Kong.

Majority entering new markets

With economic development and consumer purchasing power rising in many countries, new markets are an important source of growth. Three out of four CEOs told us they intend to actively enter new markets. This intent holds true for CEOs in emerging (72 percent) and established (76 percent) economies and for companies of all sizes.

Global integration via M&A, especially by outperformers

Sixty-six percent of CEOs plan to use mergers and acquisitions (M&A) as part of their global integration strategies. They described M&A as a key way to rapidly expand global reach – integrating new capabilities, knowledge and assets and gaining access to new customers. Interestingly, outperformers are 55 percent more likely to use M&A than underperformers, challenging the preconception that M&A is a risky and often unsuccessful strategy.[18] Prior research suggests that frequent acquirers often become extremely effective at M&A and can use it more successfully.[19]

Business designs with more global focus

As we discussed individual optimization choices with CEOs, we found that decisions and plans in one area were often related to those in other areas. Their responses formed an interlinked pattern or design, not a series of independent judgments.

Using data clustering techniques, we found four common approaches to global integration, as described in Figure 9. More than 60 percent of CEOs are implementing a globally oriented strategy; the remainder are using either a local or blended approach.

FIGURE 9 **CEO RESPONSES FALL INTO FOUR DISTINCT CLUSTERS**
The two most common approaches are more global. One focuses locally. And the fourth falls in the middle.

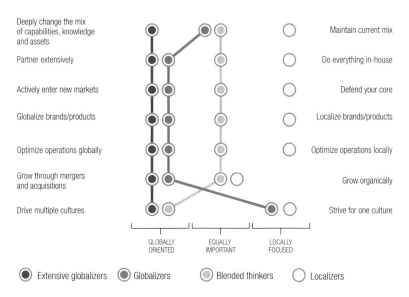

Global clusters include more outperformers

Examining the clusters more closely, we found a higher percentage of outperformers in the two globally oriented ones.[20] The similarity of the two outperforming clusters implies that CEOs of more financially successful companies have a particular business design in mind. They are partnering extensively to leverage global expertise, actively entering new markets, globally optimizing their brands, products and operations, and using mergers and acquisitions to grow their businesses and expand their capabilities globally.

FIGURE 10 **OUTPERFORMERS GRAVITATE TOWARD GLOBAL BUSINESS DESIGNS**
More outperformers are found in the two globally oriented clusters.

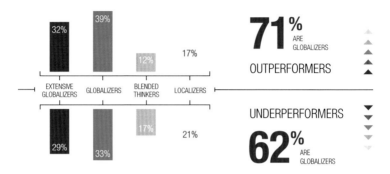

Need for carefully calibrated business design

From our discussions, it is also clear that CEOs' approaches to global integration and optimization are carefully tailored to their businesses. For example, global brands and products must have local relevance. As one telecommunications CEO put it, "We need to build and maintain global product platforms to preserve economies of scale – but we need to localize features to suit local tastes."

"Products have to be local with a global brand. I see us as a globally integrated organization with a local presence and localized products."

Georg Bauer, CEO,
BMW Financial Services

CEOs told us the case for global optimization of back-office functions such as finance and HR is clear-cut. But optimization of core production processes varies. For example, manufacturing of products that are heavy, bulky or impossible to ship may need to be optimized locally. Sales and go-to-market processes may require local knowledge and expertise. One CEO from Italy explained, "Our business model is based upon consolidation and globalization of back-office operations to reach critical mass and localization on business-specific components closely related to local markets."

CEOs also stressed the importance of having a common corporate culture, while sustaining the diversity of local geographic cultures. "The key for doing business abroad is not to seek homogeneity," one CEO from Japan observed. "Instead, we must be able to work effectively with people of different cultures and from different countries. We can learn this by working collaboratively with them."

IMPLICATIONS

Even if an Enterprise of the Future never "goes global," it still understands the capabilities available – and the competitors emerging – worldwide. Here are some ways it capitalizes on global integration opportunities:

Integrates capabilities globally to differentiate. The Enterprise of the Future searches worldwide for sources of expertise, resources and assets that can help it differentiate. Finding the right capabilities is much more important than finding the cheapest. These centers of excellence are integrated globally so that the best capabilities, knowledge and assets can be used wherever required.

Builds a carefully calibrated global business design. The Enterprise of the Future crafts its globally integrated and optimized business design based on its particular mix of capabilities, industries and geographies. It has a strategic plan for which capabilities to keep in-house and where it will partner or acquire. And when it does acquire, it knows how to manage the acquisition so that anticipated benefits are fully realized.

Finds and eliminates integration barriers. Flexible assets allow the Enterprise of the Future to be more agile in the marketplace. Location decisions are based on market and operational needs, not dictated by property deeds or restrictive leasing arrangements. Modular information technology, such as service-oriented architectures, enables rapid responses to new products and services opportunities and faster integration of new partners.

Grooms global leaders. In the Enterprise of the Future, global management development programs identify high-potential candidates throughout the company, not just from headquarters. These programs take future leaders through multiple global experiences, exposing them to a variety of cultures and markets.

Recognizes the importance of social connections within and across organizations. Social networking and real-time collaboration tools improve communication and close the distance between people in different locations. Good ideas develop and spread quicker, and problems are solved faster.

ARE YOU READY?

- Are you effectively integrating differentiating capabilities, knowledge and assets from around the world into networked centers of excellence?

- Does your organization have a globally integrated business design (even if it does not have a global footprint)?

- Do you have a detailed plan for global partnering and M&A?

- Are you developing leaders that think and act globally?

- Do you nurture and support social connections to improve integration and innovation?

CASE STUDY
LI & FUNG LIMITED: GROWTH VIA GLOBAL INTEGRATION

With a network of 10,000 suppliers and staff in 40 different countries, Hong Kong-based Li & Fung Limited can source from virtually anywhere in the world and build customized solutions for its retail customers.[21] Cotton can be purchased from America, knitted and dyed in Pakistan and sewn into garments in Cambodia – whatever configuration yields the best end result. Interestingly, the company orchestrates the supply chain for each of its customers without owning any piece of it.

Li & Fung has steadily moved up the value chain, changing its capability and asset mix to provide more sophisticated – and more profitable – services. To provide product design and brand development services in its largest market, the US, the company has established a significant onshore presence. This move is just one more example of Li & Fung's ability to be both locally relevant and globally optimized.

Acquisitions – more than 20 in less than ten years – are a key way Li & Fung grows market share in target geographic markets.[22] Typically, it preserves the front-end customer interface, which is often the reason for the acquisition, but merges the back end with its own operation within 100 days of deal close.[23] Li & Fung Limited's global integration formula certainly seems to work – between 1992 and 2006 revenues grew at a compound annual growth rate of more than 22 percent.[24]

Disruptive by nature

Most CEOs are embarking on extensive business model innovation. And outperformers are pursuing even more disruptive business model innovations than their underperforming peers. But will these bold moves pay off? What will it take to truly differentiate?

Technology enables broader business model possibilities

CEOs told us they are changing their business models because it is increasingly difficult to differentiate based on products and services alone. But they also stressed another reason – they simply have more options now.

FIGURE 11 **CEOS ARE MAKING MAJOR BUSINESS MODEL CHANGES**
Virtually all CEOs are adapting their business models – two thirds are implementing extensive innovations.

As one US CEO explained, "We're starting to think about things we couldn't do before." With the Internet, businesses can now find niche markets for rare, surplus or highly specialized goods – a virtual "garage sale," as it's often called. Business processes, as well as some products and services, are becoming more virtual. New delivery channels and electronic methods of distribution are overturning traditional industry conventions. And these advances are not just changing the way individual companies work – they're creating entirely new industries.

Enterprise model innovation most common

We also explored the different types of business model innovation CEOs are implementing. In particular, we asked about enterprise model, revenue model and industry model innovation.

> **Enterprise model** – Specializing and reconfiguring the business to deliver greater value by rethinking what is done in-house and through collaboration (as Cisco has done by focusing on brand and design while relying on partners for manufacturing, distribution and more).
>
> **Revenue model** – Changing how revenue is generated through new value propositions and new pricing models (as Gillette did by switching the primary revenue stream from razors to blades).
>
> **Industry model** – Redefining an existing industry, moving into a different industry or creating an entirely new one (think music industry and the Apple iPod and iTunes).[25]

Among those making extensive changes to their business models, enterprise model innovation is the dominant choice. Forty-four percent of CEOs are focused solely on enterprise model innovation or are implementing it in combination with other forms of business model innovation. This trend toward enterprise model innovation is even more pronounced in emerging economies (53 percent).

FIGURE 12 **ENTERPRISE MODEL INNOVATION IS MOST PREVALENT**
CEOs are largely focused on reconfiguring their businesses to specialize and collaborate.

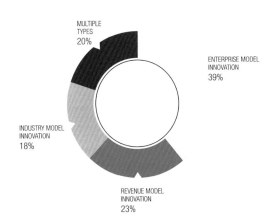

MULTIPLE TYPES
20%

ENTERPRISE MODEL INNOVATION
39%

INDUSTRY MODEL INNOVATION
18%

REVENUE MODEL INNOVATION
23%

Collaboration imperative drives enterprise model innovation

The main message we heard from proponents of enterprise model innovation is that going solo is increasingly difficult. "We're very vertically challenged," one electronics CEO said when describing the difficulty of owning the entire value chain.

CEOs can no longer afford to invest money and scarce management resources in activities that are not differentiating. They intend to specialize. One US CEO explained, "We have to collaborate to survive; there are fewer things that will be cost-effective to do on our own. We will continue to do less inside the organization and more with partners and even competitors."

"For us, enterprise model innovation is primarily about having the right business model to enter other markets and secure new capabilities."
Andrew Brandler, CEO, CLP Holding Limited

While 38 percent of CEOs plan to keep work within their organizations, 71 percent – nearly twice as many – plan to focus on collaboration and partnerships. CEOs told us they are pursuing more collaborative models to gain efficiencies, fend off competitive threats and avoid commoditization. Their end goal is to offer customers a differentiated value proposition. "The notion of what comprises an 'enterprise' is critical. It must be a loosely coupled system," said one public sector leader from Australia. "It's about deciding when to collaborate, whom to involve, how to lessen the destructive force of competition."

Revenue model innovators shift the value mix

Among those pursuing revenue model innovations, nine out of ten are reconfiguring the product, service and value mix. Half are working on new pricing structures.

CEOs are incorporating more services into their offering portfolios and changing one-time payment models to ones centered on recurring charges. More are starting to price based on value to the customer, rather than on cost-plus. Depending on the particular needs of their respective industries, some companies are bundling to create more valuable solutions, while others are unbundling to offer customers a menu of choices. At the same time, "customers are getting better educated on global pricing, driving a need for more transparency," one CEO from Sweden explained. "Product pricing is moving from reactive to proactive as a result."

"We have become much smarter in how we do our pricing. Our pricing model is now based on customer segmentation and value created for those customers."
Steffen Schiottz-Christensen, Managing Director, Maersk Logistics North Asia

Interestingly, CEOs are also using revenue model innovation as part of their geographic expansion strategies. Having the right pricing structure, they told us, is critical when entering markets such as China and India where consumers have a wide range of incomes.

Industry model innovation remains rare

CEOs mentioned several reasons for not pursuing industry model innovation. But most can be summed up with: It's tough to do. For similar reasons, industry model innovators are more focused on redefining their existing industries (73 percent) than on entering or creating entirely new ones (36 percent).

Extremely risk-averse industries present even more obstacles. As one pharmaceutical CEO explained, "Our industry has an 'innovation paradox.' We are constantly driving for innovation on the one hand, while being risk averse on the other. Pharma companies still hope for the 'blockbuster party,' and they are trapped within that model. The company that breaks through this will be the winner, and others will follow."

Some CEOs do not believe their companies have the appropriate position in their industries or within their own value chains to drive this kind of significant change. But a few do. They are the industry leaders who ask: If not us, then who?

> "When the business model is innovative, operations and the product will follow automatically."
> *Ronald de Jong, CEO*
> *Philips CL, Germany*

Outperformers take on the industry model challenge

Consistent with the overall sample, outperformers are very interested in enterprise model innovation. But they are also planning 40 percent more industry model innovation than underperformers.[26] The question is: Are these outperformers pursuing more industry model innovation because they have the clout to do so? Or are they outperformers because of their insight and inclination to question industry norms? From our CEO conversations, we're convinced it's actually both – a reinforcing cycle. Innovation successes can provide the financial means and industry position to attempt bolder moves, which, in turn, can improve business performance.

FIGURE 13 **OUTPERFORMERS ARE MORE LIKELY TO PURSUE INDUSTRY MODEL INNOVATION**
In general, outperformers seem more willing to attempt the most difficult type of business model change – industry model innovation.

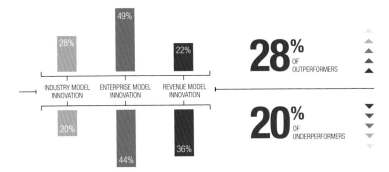

IMPLICATIONS

The Enterprise of the Future constantly searches for new ways to compete. Here are some ideas on how it develops a disruptive mindset:

Thinks like an outsider. The Enterprise of the Future does blue-sky, green-field thinking. Its goal is to spark innovation by thinking about "starting over from scratch." It finds ways to work with people and organizations that are not part of the industry status quo to develop new models. It challenges every assumption of its business model – just as an outsider would.

Draws breakthrough ideas from other industries. The Enterprise of the Future is a student of other industries because it realizes that game-changing plays spread like wildfire. It scours customer and technology trends that are transforming other sectors and segments of the market and considers how they could be applied to its own industry and business model.

Empowers entrepreneurs. The Enterprise of the Future understands the challenges of achieving business model innovation from within. It empowers its entrepreneurs with support, funding and freedom to drive disruptive change, which may threaten competitors' models – and even its own.

Experiments creatively in the market, not just the lab. The Enterprise of the Future often pilots models in the marketplace, obtaining real-time feedback and making iterative adjustments. It even uses virtual worlds – such as Second Life – to "test" models and apply what it learns to its "real life" business.

Manages today's business while experimenting with tomorrow's model. New business models are often at odds with established ones, creating inherent tension within the organization. Even if the models are not directed at the same customers, they are still competing for resources and attention. The Enterprise of the Future actively manages these potential conflicts so that it can try out bold business model innovations, while ensuring business as usual delivers results.

ARE YOU READY?

- Is a disruptive business model about to transform your industry? Is it more likely to come from you or your competitors?

- Do you spend time thinking about where the next disruption will come from?

- Are you watching other industries for concepts and business models that could transform your market?

- Are you able to create space for entrepreneurs and innovative business models while continuing to drive performance today?

CASE STUDY
ELI LILLY AND COMPANY: BUILDING PIPELINE THROUGH
COLLABORATIVE BUSINESS MODELS

To bring new medicines to market faster, US pharmaceutical maker Eli Lilly and Company integrates an extensive network of external partners through its constantly evolving collaborative business models. In 2001, for example, Lilly launched InnoCentive, an open marketplace for innovation. On this website, "seeker" organizations anonymously submit scientific challenges to a diverse crowd of more than 140,000 "solvers" from 175 countries.[27] The best solutions can earn financial awards of up to $US1 million. Lilly has since spun off InnoCentive, but still retains partial ownership in the venture.

More recently, Lilly has embarked on another business model innovation – establishing itself as a Fully Integrated Pharmaceutical Network (FIPNet). The FIPNet model is based on pioneering risk-sharing relationships, such as its 2007 agreement with Nicholas Piramal India Limited (NPIL).[28] Under this contract, NPIL will develop one of Lilly's molecules at its own expense, from preclinical work to early clinical trials. If NPIL is successful and the compound reaches the second stage of human testing, Lilly can reacquire it in exchange for certain milestone payments and royalties.

These collaborative business models offer several benefits: reducing costs; increasing development capacity; accelerating the drug development process; and better leveraging both Lilly's assets and those of its external partners. Lilly's results speak for themselves – between 2002 and 2007 sales increased at a compound annual growth rate of 11 percent.[29]

Genuine, not just generous

An emerging generation of socially minded customers, workers, partners, activists and investors is watching virtually every move companies make. Recognizing this, CEOs are investing rapidly in corporate social responsibility (CSR). But how far will they go?

Ceos struggle to meet rapidly increasing CSR expectations

CEOs generally agree that customer expectations of CSR are increasing. The environment is one obvious touchstone – climate change has become an urgent call to action for citizens and companies around the world. And it has sensitized both citizens and corporations to the wide array of environmental and social issues – from child labor to recycling to product safety – that they can do something about.

While customers have always cared about societal issues, their concerns are now more frequently turning into action and influencing purchasing decisions. According to a recent CSR study, 75 percent of the companies surveyed say that the number of advocacy groups collecting and reporting CSR-related information on them has increased over the past three years.[30]

Meanwhile, many CEOs are struggling to put CSR into practice. "We talk too much, and don't do anything about increasing customer expectations of corporate social responsibility," admitted one financial services CEO.

CSR-related factors rising on CEO agenda

Across our previous CEO studies, only three external forces have consistently ranked higher in each consecutive survey: socioeconomic factors; environmental issues; and people skills. Interestingly, all three are linked to CSR.

FIGURE 14 **COINCIDENCE OR FORESHADOWING?**
Of the nine change drivers we discuss with CEOs in each survey, only three continue to rise in importance.

PERCENTAGE OF CEOS SELECTING AS A TOP CHANGE DRIVER

2004   2006   2008

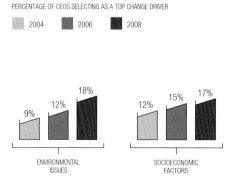

ENVIRONMENTAL ISSUES: 9%, 12%, 18%

SOCIOECONOMIC FACTORS: 12%, 15%, 17%

PEOPLE SKILLS: 42%, 44%, 48%

With talent in short supply, employers' CSR reputations are an important tool to attract and retain employees. Companies are also recognizing that they are being held mutually accountable, along with the public sector, for the socioeconomic well-being of the regions in which they operate.

CEO concern about environmental issues has doubled over the past four years globally. However, this concern is not evenly distributed. CEOs in the Americas are beginning to show more interest, but focus is increasing faster among European CEOs. Asia Pacific showed the most dramatic increase, with attention nearly tripling since 2004.

Regulatory compliance, however, is not CEOs' chief concern. As one public sector leader from France points out, "Environmental legislation is less of a problem. It is reasonably easy to be ISO 14000 certified. It is much harder to face media and political pressure from socially active environmental NGOs."

FIGURE 15 **THE CEO AGENDA IS GOING GREEN**
Concern about the environment has grown significantly over the past four years – especially in Asia Pacific.

PERCENT OF CEOs RATING ENVIRONMENTAL FACTORS AS A TOP CHANGE DRIVER GLOBALLY

2004 — 9%
2006 — 12%
2008 — 18%

CEOs see opportunities not threats

CEOs are clearly conscious of their obligation to "do no harm" and are painfully aware of the regulators and non-governmental organizations (NGOs) monitoring their every step. But they also see opportunity in CSR.

CEOs talked about how CSR affects their brands – both at home and in new markets. "Corporate identity and CSR will play an important role in differentiating a company in the future," one electronics CEO said. "This will make a big difference in new markets such as Russia and other Eastern European markets."

They also described how CSR is affecting their top and bottom lines. "Our organization is responding aggressively to green issues in the marketplace, which have become the focus of several of our key customer segments," one US CEO told us. "We are introducing new green-based insurance products into the market."

CEOs were also quick to point out that CSR is critical to maintaining market share. "Consumers will increasingly make choices based on the sources of the products they buy, even the ingredients and processes used in making these products," said one consumer products CEO.

"Our strong commitment to corporate sustainability will be a clear differentiator for us with all stakeholders."

Tom Johnstone, CEO, SKF

FIGURE 16 **CSR: OBLIGATION OR OPPORTUNITY?**
CEOs are generally positive about the impact of rising CSR expectations and are increasing their investment in this area rapidly.[31]

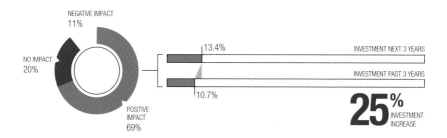

New products and services top of mind for CSR-focused CEOs

For the moment, it seems that CEOs who focus on CSR issues invest more in new products and services than other CEOs. This is perhaps a sign that the initial market and consumer focus is on "socially responsible" and "green" products and services. Over time, we believe companies' CSR focus will expand beyond new products and services to a broader enterprise "footprint" – the impact they have on the societies in which they operate.

FIGURE 17 **CSR-FOCUSED CEOS ARE ENTHUSIASTIC ABOUT NEW PRODUCT POSSIBILITIES**
The focus areas of these CEOs hold a couple of surprises. They're very interested in new product and service opportunities for socially aware customers. However, transparency is not a top priority.

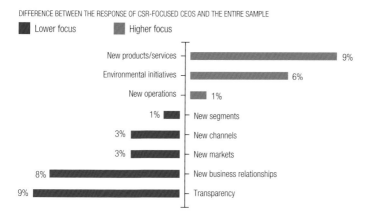

Largest investment increase in CSR

Although current CSR investment levels are modest compared with the other customer trends we asked about, CEOs plan to spend more over the next three years. Their CSR investments will grow by 25 percent, which is faster than the other trends we discussed – rising prosperity in rapidly developing and developed economies, and informed and collaborative customers. Interestingly, this pattern holds true even among emerging market CEOs (with a 22 percent increase). One CEO from China told us, "Over the last three years, we have invested twice as much in CSR and environment initiatives as we have in the previous 30 years combined."

> "Our company is investing extensively in corporate social responsibility. We need to be a reference in this domain. As the leader of the luxury industry, we have to stay ahead."
>
> *Yves Carcelle, Chairman and CEO, Louis Vuitton*

IMPLICATIONS

Many CEOs are already moving beyond doing good and are growing their businesses by being more socially responsible. Here are some ways the Enterprise of the Future approaches CSR even more holistically:

Understands CSR expectations. Too many companies find themselves relying on assumptions about what CSR means to their customers. Only one quarter of the companies surveyed in a recent CSR study said they understood customers' concerns well.[32] However, the Enterprise of the Future knows what its customers expect. It uses facts and direct customer input as the basis for its decisions.

Informs but does not overwhelm. The Enterprise of the Future is transparent, but unobtrusive. It finds creative ways to provide relevant information, such as codes on packaging that allow interested customers to look up details – sourcing information, potential environmental impact and recycling instructions – while in the store or later at home.

Starts with green. Given the price of oil and rising concern over carbon emissions, energy efficiency is critical for businesses as well as our planet. The Enterprise of the Future often begins its CSR changes with environmental initiatives. Through these efforts, it learns more about how to effectively collaborate on issues that affect us all.

Involves NGOs as part of the solution. Instead of being wary of activist groups – or simply reporting data to them – the Enterprise of the Future collaborates with them. For instance, it might enlist NGOs to help monitor and inspect facilities or to assist in establishing industry standards.

Makes work part of making the world a better place. Prospective and existing employees want to work for ethical, socially responsible organizations. But the Enterprise of the Future understands that workers also want to be personally involved in solving CSR issues. Its initiatives rally employees together in a cause that literally makes the world a better place.

ARE YOU READY?

- Do you understand your customers' CSR expectations? How are you involving them in solutions?

- Do you know which NGOs your customers listen to? Are you collaborating with those groups?

- Have you gained insights from green initiatives that can be applied to your broader corporate social responsibility strategy?

- Are you offering employees the opportunity to personally make a difference?

- How do you ensure that actions taken throughout the enterprise – and the extended value chain – are consistent with your CSR values and stated policies?

CASE STUDY
MARKS & SPENCER: SERIOUS ABOUT SOCIAL RESPONSIBILITY

To meet growing corporate social responsibility expectations, British retailer Marks & Spencer (M&S) has embarked on a £200 million, five-year plan that affects almost every aspect of its operations.

When this effort was launched in 2006, the retailer knew it needed to engage customers in solving issues, not simply provide them with information. As one example, it gave shoppers bags "for life." If one wore out, its replacement was free. After four weeks, the retailer began charging for plastic bags, donating the proceeds to environmental charities. Very quickly, customers began re-evaluating whether they really needed a plastic bag. Even though the few cents didn't matter much financially, the fee made people stop and think.

Behind the retailer's 35,000 products sit 2,000 factories, more than 20,000 farms, fisheries and forests, and an estimated 500,000 workers in the developing world. Through its recently established online supplier exchange, the company strives to simultaneously improve efficiency and sustainability. For instance, farmers who create biogases from farm waste are now selling green electricity to M&S – along with their beef.

M&S has proved it's possible to do well while doing good: The company's operating profit has increased at a compound annual growth rate of more than 14 percent over the past five years.[33]

Building your Enterprise of the Future

Thoughts and views on the future of business are evolving quickly. We feel privileged to bring together the emerging thinking of so many CEOs worldwide. Their collective wisdom points to an Enterprise of the Future that is: hungry for change; innovative beyond customer imagination; globally integrated; disruptive by nature; and genuine, not just generous.

But there is one more attribute evident in CEOs' responses. Despite the challenges and issues it faces, the Enterprise of the Future is fundamentally optimistic. The CEOs we spoke with are upbeat – not just about opportunities for their organizations (important as that is), but also about the broader outlook for business and society.

ACKNOWLEDGMENTS

We would like to thank the 1,130 CEOs, general managers and senior public sector and business leaders from around the world who generously shared hours of time and years of experience with us. Their compelling insights and enthusiasm about the Enterprise of the Future were truly invaluable and inspiring. In particular, we appreciate the CEOs who allowed us to include quotes from their interviews to highlight key thoughts and messages.

We would also like to acknowledge the contributions of the IBM team that worked on *The Enterprise of the Future*:

Leadership Team: Peter Korsten (Study Executive Leader), Saul Berman, Marc Chapman, Steven Davidson, Rainer Mehl and George Pohle;

Project Team: Phaedra Kortekaas (Study Director), Denise Arnette, Steve Ballou, Ragna Bell, Amy Blitz, Angie Casey, Sally Drayton, Christine Kinser, Keith Landis, Kathleen Martin and Magesh Vaidheeswaran;

And the hundreds of IBM Leaders worldwide who conducted the in-person CEO interviews.

REFERENCES

1 For readability, we refer to this collective group as "CEOs" throughout. IBM leaders conducted more than 95 percent of these interviews face to face. The Economist Intelligence Unit administered the remainder by telephone.

2 Based on availability of financial information, we were able to include 530 companies in our financial analysis. For analytical and statistical reasons, we compared performance on three financial benchmarks: revenue compound annual growth rate (CAGR) 2003-2006; net profit margin CAGR 2003-2006; and absolute profit margin average for 2003 and 2006.

3 Market factors typically include market dynamics, competition and customer behavior.

4 Based on revenue CAGR 2003-2006.

5 This finding is from an IBM study called "Making Change Work," which analyzes change management practices based on input from more than 1,400 change managers from around the world.

6 "Strong 2007 Results on Continued Growth and Operational Improvement." ABB press release. February 14, 2008. http://www.abb.com/cawp/seitp202/402891eccf6 a8cdcc12573e20038dd15.aspx

7 In our survey, the term "total investments" was defined as all asset investments plus investment in research and development, marketing and sales.

8 "2007 Was the Year of the 'Omni Consumer' According to IBM Analysis." IBM press release. December 17, 2007.

9 In our survey, the term "total investments" was defined as all asset investments plus investment in research and development, marketing and sales.

10 Based on net profit margin CAGR 2003-2006.

11 Based on revenue CAGR 2003-2006.

12 IBM analysis.

13 "Nintendo Rewards Its Customers with New Loyalty Program." Xbox Solution. December 11, 2003. http://talk.xboxsolution.com/showthread.php?t=1088

14 "Casual Gamers Help Nintendo Wii Take Lead in 2008, says iSuppli." Tekrati. February 14, 2008. http://ce.tekrati.com/research/10080/

15 "Worldwide Hardware Shipments." VGChartz.com. Accessed March 27, 2008.

16 Based on net profit margin CAGR 2003-2006.

17 "Expanding the Innovation Horizon: The Global CEO Study 2006." IBM Global Business Services. March 2006. http://www.ibm.com/services/ceo2006

18 Based on net profit margin CAGR 2003-2006.

19 Kapur, Vivek, Jeffere Ferris and John Juliano. "The growth triathlon: Growth via course, capability and conviction." IBM Institute for Business Value. December 2004.

20 Based on absolute profit margin average for 2003 and 2006.

21 Li & Fung Group website. http://www.lifunggroup.com/front.html; "Global Reach, Local Presence." Li & Fung Limited. http://www.lifung.com/eng/network/map.php

22 Li & Fung press releases, 1999-2007.

23 Voxant FD Wire. "Li & Fung Limited – Acquisition of KarstadtQuelle Sourcing Arm – Conference Call – Final." October 2, 2006. IBM interview with Victor Fung, March 2008.

24 Li & Fung Limited, 2006 annual report.

25 For more information about business model innovation, see: Giesen, Edward, Saul J. Berman, Ragna Bell and Amy Blitz. "Paths to success: Three ways to innovate your business model." IBM Institute for Business Value. June 2007.

26 Based on absolute profit margin average for 2003 and 2006.

27 The InnoCentive website. http://www.innocentive.com/

28 "Nicholas Piramal Announces Drug Development Agreement with Eli Lilly and Company: Collaboration Represents a New Clinical Development Model." Nicholas Piramal India Limited press release. January 12, 2007. http://piramalhealthcare. com/UploadedImages/pressrelease_files/PR-Lilly-R&D-agreement.pdf

29 Eli Lilly and Company 2002 and 2007 annual reports.

30 Pohle, George and Jeff Hittner. "Attaining sustainable growth through corporate social responsibility." IBM Institute for Business Value. February 2008.

31 In our survey, the term "total investments" was defined as all asset investments plus investment in research and development, marketing and sales.

32 Pohle, George and Jeff Hittner. Op. cit.

33 Marks & Spencer 2006 and 2007 annual reports.

Succeeding in the new economic environment

Focus on value, opportunity, speed

Saul Berman, Steven Davidson,
Sara Longworth and Amy Blitz

The global financial crisis of 2008-09 unleashed sudden
and sweeping economic change in the world economy.
A major transformation is under way and "business as usual"
responses are unlikely to succeed. Based on our experience, our
previous studies and an analysis of early winners from the global
financial crisis and longer-term winners from previous economic
transformations, we advise CEOs and business leaders to focus
more than ever on value, to exploit opportunities presented by
the new economic environment and to act on both quickly.

The tremendous uncertainty generated by the global financial crisis has created
an urgent need for action. This chapter offers our perspective on what business
leaders need to do to succeed in the new economic environment. To provide guidance, we have identified patterns in the chaos of economic transformations such
as the current one.[1] On the gloomy side, many companies without sufficient cash
reserves or fundamental strength do not survive such periods, as we have seen
with the dramatic collapse, bankruptcy or threatened bankruptcy of seemingly
rock-solid companies in financial services, retail, real estate, automotive and other
sectors, starting with Bear Stearns and Lehman Brothers and cascading through
the world economy. This trend is global, with many manufacturing companies, for

example, closing in Shenzhen, China, and US, European, Japanese and Korean auto manufacturers taking huge losses.[2] And many other troubled companies are being exposed in diverse sectors in Europe, Asia and North America.

On the positive side, history shows that even periods of tremendous dislocation produce winners.[3] In the panic of the 1870s – a period similar to the present, with a mortgage bubble leading to a financial collapse and an extreme tightening of credit – those with cash, like Rockefeller, Gould and Carnegie in the United States, seized opportunities to establish dominance in oil, steel, railroads and other emerging industries.[4] And while some financial institutions collapsed, a new generation of innovative banks such as Deutsche Bank was established on the back of the new industries.[5] Likewise, during the 1930s, those who succeeded targeted the emerging industries of that era, notably movies, radio, automotive and electricity. Today, many of the early winners are focused on value-oriented customers, entertainment and sectors such as life sciences, telecommunications and the environment, as well as "flight" sectors such as gold.[6]

LESSONS FROM EARLY WINNERS

Businesses that are performing well – even in these economic straits – are employing three common strategies: focusing on value, exploiting opportunity and acting quickly.

What separates the winners from the rest of the pack in times like these? What strategies and characteristics can be emulated and applied today across diverse industries, regions and competitive positions? To help answer these questions, we identified early winners in the current period, beginning with large US-listed companies whose stock appreciated by at least 5 percent in 2008, at a time when the S&P 500 index declined by 37 percent.[7] In all, 61 companies emerged as early winners. Demonstrating the power of strategy over industry trends, these companies span diverse sectors, with 31 percent in services, 22 percent in financial services, 12 percent in health care and 12 percent in basic materials, followed by energy, capital goods, utilities and transportation. Moreover, those who won in 2008, won big, with their stock appreciating by an average of 24 percent, well above our 5 percent hurdle.

We then studied each of these companies and the strategies that led to their success. From this, we identified patterns in their strategies that allowed these companies to not only survive the economic transformation but to thrive in it. We then looked beyond this group of standouts to companies that performed well in Europe and Asia in 2008 and found that similar patterns applied. In brief, early winners focus on value, exploit opportunity and act quickly (see Figure 1).

While some of the early winners were simply in the right place at the right time (notably a few gold companies), most demonstrate the power of having a strategic vision that can thrive in even the toughest of times. Overall, the early winners:

Focus on value via sustainable strategies that emphasize long-term value. For example, the Dutch Rabobank Group, along with several other commercial banks in our 2008 data sample, performed well by avoiding high-profit, high-

FIGURE 1 **FIRMS THAT OUTPERFORMED THE S&P 500 IN 2008 SHARE THREE COMMON STRATEGIES**

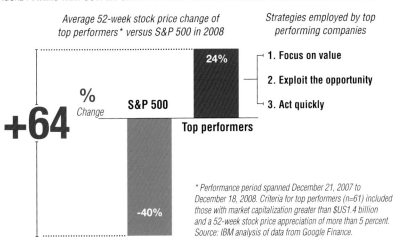

Average 52-week stock price change of top performers* versus S&P 500 in 2008

Strategies employed by top performing companies

24%

% Change

S&P 500

Top performers

-40%

+64

1. Focus on value

2. Exploit the opportunity

3. Act quickly

* Performance period spanned December 21, 2007 to December 18, 2008. Criteria for top performers (n=61) included those with market capitalization greater than $US1.4 billion and a 52-week stock price appreciation of more than 5 percent. Source: IBM analysis of data from Google Finance.

risk offerings such as sub-prime mortgages, instead holding to low-risk lending principles.[8] Companies targeting value-oriented customers also did well. While several including McDonald's provide offerings at very low prices, others such as Netflix and Strayer Education (an online service) are using technology in innovative ways to slash prices through revolutionary new business models.[9]

Exploit opportunities presented during downturns, including growing through low-cost acquisitions and stock buy-backs. Another key area of opportunity is growth through innovation, transforming existing industries or introducing new offerings in emerging industries. Early winners in this area spanned life sciences/biotech, electronics, environmental quality and telecommunications. For example, Japan's Nippon Telegraph and Telephone continued to introduce groundbreaking innovations in its broadband services and mobile communications offerings in 2008, including the world launch of its Next Generation Network, which aims to provide ubiquitous services on full IP-network infrastructures.[10]

Act quickly, with the agility to respond ahead of, or at least to keep pace with, rapid changes in the new economic environment. Barclays, for example, acted swiftly – leaping regulatory and other hurdles – to acquire Lehman Brothers assets by September 23, 2008, just days after Lehman's September 14 collapse. Within hours of the acquisition, the screens wrapped around 745 Seventh Avenue in Manhattan switched from the Lehman name to Barclays' blue logo.[11] Equally decisive was Tesco's move in 2008 to introduce a new Discount Brand line to avoid losing customers to lower-cost competitors.[12]

Based on our analysis and experience, as well as several of our previous studies on related topics, we can define key elements of these three strategies successful companies deploy well in times of uncertainty (see Figure 2).

FIGURE 2 **TO THRIVE, NOT JUST SURVIVE, COMPANIES NEED TO TAKE ACTION ON THREE FRONTS**

Focus on value	Exploit opportunities	Act with speed
1 Do more with less • Cut costs strategically • Conserve working capital • Protect cash reserves • Increase flexibility, responsiveness **2 Focus on the core** • Create value for clients • Reduce non-core costs • Shift from fixed to variable costs **3 Understand your customers** • Target value-oriented customers • Reduce complexity	**1 Capture share** • Disrupt weaker competitors • Focus on growth markets • Acquire bargain-priced assets **2 Build future capabilities** • Protect and acquire critical talent • Establish corporate infrastructure for growth • Invest in innovation **3 Change your industry** • Understand your place in new environment • Pioneer new industry approaches • Exploit new revenue models • Cultivate strategic partnerships	**1 Manage change** • Overcome the "change gap" **2 Empower leaders** • Establish strong, aligned leadership • Communicate strategy clearly and often **3 Manage risk** • Reduce risk and increase transparency

Source: IBM Institute for Business Value.

FOCUS ON VALUE

1 Do more with less

Cut costs strategically. Traditional approaches often involve spreading the pain of cost reductions evenly across business units and geographies. This may seem fair and might minimize disputes within the management team, but it avoids the difficult and important decisions that will drive future success. Significant cost reductions are better accomplished through more strategic decisions to exit whole activities, businesses or markets. Both revenue and cost need to be considered. Leaders need to preserve key investments that will drive future growth. For example, many global companies are driving higher cost-reduction targets in mature markets in order to invest more heavily in emerging markets. Others are considering significant business model innovations involving, for example, more partnering or outsourcing to provide upfront savings and greater flexibility. For those with a global presence, now is the time to drive robust optimization efforts to bring down costs by locating activities in the right place using the right level of resources and slashing duplication. Figure 3 shows how companies can take a more strategic approach to cutting costs, increasing revenue and improving profits.

How and where companies cut costs has a long-term effect – far beyond the current downturn.

Conserve working capital. Clearly, given current restrictions on credit, companies need to focus on reducing working capital in their businesses if they have not done so already. Managing working capital involves driving down inventories, accounts receivable and accounts payable. Inventory analysis needs to examine each item's profitability, its value to the company, as well as the associated variability, velocity and volume, to enable significant inventory reductions. Addressing accounts receivables can improve cash management by, for example, adjusting processes to focus on accounts that often pay late versus those that pay on time.

FIGURE 3 **COST-REDUCTION OPPORTUNITIES SHOULD BE EVALUATED IN A STRATEGIC CONTEXT**

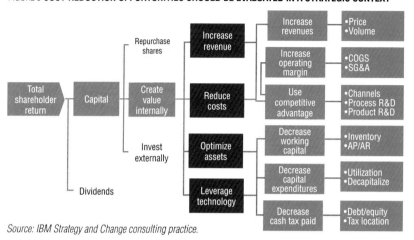

Source: IBM Strategy and Change consulting practice.

Protect cash reserves. In a credit crisis, cash is central to survival and strategic flexibility. It serves as a buffer against lean times and enables the strategic acquisition of undervalued, perhaps even bargain-priced, assets. Of course, companies that do not have strong cash reserves today cannot reinvent history to create them; but a value-based reassessment of the portfolio may reveal opportunities to generate a greater return through divestment or liquidation, especially when weighed against investment opportunities to improve or expand core businesses. Leaders should also explore alliances or partnerships that provide access to cash or cost-effective capabilities, particularly if their preferred strategies require significant investment.

Increase flexibility and responsiveness. Companies must understand how vulnerable they are to declines in demand and revenues, and develop the flexibility in their capacity and cost base in order to cope. They need to engage in active scenario modeling to evaluate how far production cost break-even points must be lowered and capacity reduced (or used differently) to prevent losses. In doing this, companies must also plan for the upturn by avoiding cutting too deep, so that they can ramp up quickly once conditions improve. This requires a strong understanding of industry trends, competitor performance and behavior, as well as of underlying economic conditions. Companies must also develop more sophisticated sense-and-respond capabilities. In the automotive industry, for example, the Ford Motor Company has sidestepped many of the challenges facing its rivals by cutting factory capacity to match decreased demand, announcing in 2005 the closure of 17 factories and the elimination of 50,000 jobs, many through buyouts and early retirement.[13]

2 Focus on the core

Create value for clients and preserve differentiation. It is critical to cut spending on low-value activities and redeploy it to investments that generate growth, margins and true differentiation. Being able to accurately identify where value is generated at all levels of the organization – from divisions to specific products or offerings to particular customers – is an essential first step. But for those without strong financial systems or good management information, this could be a complex task. However difficult, the benefits are clear. Here again, Ford has cut costs and raised capital through borrowing and divestitures, including Jaguar, Land Rover and Aston Martin.[14] Similarly, UK grocer Waitrose has performed well in terms of customer growth by leveraging its strong reputation for high-quality food while controlling the average cost of a shopping basket through deeper discounts on commodity products.[15]

Strip out non-value-add activities and reduce non-core costs. Companies need to understand which activities contribute strategic value. As part of this, they must rethink initiatives and have more regular capital reviews. As well as "trimming the fat" on a project-by-project basis, they must consider cutting entire projects or groups of projects, allowing no "sacred cows." This approach requires a commitment to eliminate weak businesses and divest where needed, moving non-core activities to shared services or to outsourced solutions. For example, many companies are reprioritizing large-scale technology investments. They are also reducing the cost of managing today's systems to free up investment for more strategic IT projects.

Shift from fixed to variable costs. This requires a clear identification of and focus on core activities. The need for more flexible costs and capacity is leading some companies to look afresh at their business and operating models and consider outsourcing some functions that they previously chose to keep in-house. For example, a significant number of multinational companies are considering increased outsourcing of their IT development centers to India and China. More holistic sourcing strategies, from workforce management and contract labor to strategic partnering, are also key here.

Investment choices should center on activities that differentiate and drive revenue growth.

3 Understand your customers

Target value-oriented customers. Another strategy likely to succeed in this environment is to rebalance offerings to serve new, more value-oriented customers. Eight of the 61 early winners have business models that center on offering very low-cost goods and services in diverse sectors, including retail, entertainment, education and fast food. And this can be a long-term strategy for success in good times as well as in bad, as companies such as McDonald's have demonstrated.

Reduce complexity. As they focus on their core activities, companies should take the opportunity to reduce or eliminate the complexities that may have crept into their businesses during the good years, including customization or extensive variations to a product or service that the customer may not value or understand. In telecommunications and banking, for example, the pace of product and pricing innovation can outstrip an organization's ability to manage the operational complexity it creates. Companies should examine the case for simplifying product portfolios, pricing structures and the number of promotions, and cease offering customizations that customers will not pay for – even if making these changes requires investment.

ARE YOU READY?

- Have you moved to protect revenue, conserve cash and cut costs while developing and implementing a more strategic approach to such issues?

- Do you know which businesses, markets, products and customers contribute the most value, growth and profit to your business? Which are not aligned closely to your business strategy and should be cut?

- Have you reviewed and prioritized your initiatives so that you can seize the opportunities presented by the new economic environment?

- Are you making your costs more flexible? Are you considering new workforce management strategies or innovative business models to achieve this?

- Have you reassessed your partnering strategy and relationships? Are you clear about which partners are strategic and which are commodity-based?

EXPLOIT OPPORTUNITIES

1 Capture share

Disrupt weaker competitors. For those with a clear vision for their companies and industries – and the financial resources to act – the downturn will create opportunities to set the change agenda, rather than respond to someone else's, to gain share and to build key capabilities. Bold moves, disruptive strategies and positioning to win in a globally integrated economy are all part of the path to success. Reaching out to and understanding the needs of customers, both existing ones and those who may consider shifting from competitors in such unusual times, will be an important element of the strategy. Business partners should also reassure customers that they are allies in this era, seeking to help reduce the impact of market uncertainty. A friend in need is a friend for the long term. And before considering strategies such as developing lower-cost products with fewer features, it is important to understand what the customer truly wants.

Focus efforts on growth markets. For companies seeking growth, markets in Asia, Central and Eastern Europe, the Middle East and Latin America are proving fertile ground, offering stronger opportunities for expansion than mature markets in Western Europe or North America. IBM, for example, has performed very well by shifting its relative focus to growth markets in recent years. Its newly established growth markets unit generated more than twice the revenue growth of IBM's major markets operations in 2008.[16] Similarly, Tesco has maintained strong growth at the group level by following an international portfolio approach to investment, which has generated strong gains in Hungary and Malaysia.[17] Facing slowing growth in mature markets, many business leaders are redirecting investment toward emerging markets, raising growth targets as they do so, even in these uncertain times. Many business leaders are also reviewing how they segment and organize to engage their customers, with the growth/mature market distinction becoming more important.

Acquire bargain-priced assets. Companies with significant cash reserves have the opportunity to buy attractively priced assets that support their overall strategies. Several of our early winners focused on acquisitions or stock buy-backs, taking advantage of bargains. Overall, we are seeing substantial merger and acquisition (M&A) activity throughout the global economy, particularly in financial services, such as the acquisition of Lehman Brothers segments by Nomura and Barclays in late September 2008.[18] We expect M&A activity in pharmaceuticals, as well as in other sectors. For both acquirers and targets, it is important to act quickly. For example, UK frozen food retailer Iceland profited from its acquisition of 51 Woolworths stores in January 2009 after its earlier and higher bid in 2008 was rejected.[19]

2 Build future capabilities

Protect and acquire critical talent. Despite extreme market pressures, leaders must balance the tactical concerns of today with a clear focus on the longer term. To build future capabilities, it is important to stay focused on human capital issues, such as keeping and motivating top performers, recruiting new talent at potentially lower cost and leveraging a global workforce. Top performers have the flexibility to move somewhere else if they are not convinced a company has the right strategy and execution capabilities to survive and succeed. It is important to engage these top performers, to communicate the strategy effectively and give them a role and a stake in the company's future success.

Amid economic chaos, once-in-a-lifetime opportunities often emerge.

Establish the corporate infrastructure to seize growth opportunities. When markets turn, the best returns often go to those companies that respond quickly. Recent experience has shown how long it takes to build the structures, capabilities, processes and systems to seize growth market opportunities. Now is the time to invest for the mid-term. Many Chinese companies, for example, are establishing the governance, organization structures, human capital, processes and systems to enable them to run on a truly global basis. Likewise, many banks, a sector clearly under fire, are investing in new assets and upgrading core banking systems in order to increase operational effectiveness and improve transparency for the long term. A focus on forward-looking IT investments (funded by reductions in maintenance costs for today's systems) will be essential for enabling business agility.

Invest in innovation. Several of the outperforming companies in 2008 are focused on innovation, primarily in life sciences, telecommunications, electronics and environmental quality. By carving out a niche in a downturn, companies can establish long-term dominance – a strategy IBM used effectively in the 1930s. By investing in R&D during the depths of the Great Depression, IBM was well positioned when the recovery began and customers needed complex data management systems.[20] Today's early winners – from Netflix and Nippon Telegraph and Telephone to others in life sciences/biotech and environmental quality – are already demonstrating the power of innovation in a downturn.

3 Change your industry

Understand the impact of the current transformation on your industry, and profit from it with innovative new business models. Business leaders must assess whether their industries are apt to consolidate, grow, shrink or even die. They must also understand how competitors, suppliers, consumers and others are responding to the economic changes, and whether barriers to entry are increasing or decreasing. From this analysis, business leaders should gain insight into where opportunities for new business models exist. Two thirds of the CEOs who participated in the Global CEO Study are implementing significant business model innovations; Figure 4 outlines the types of business model innovation they are pursuing.

Pioneer new industry approaches and standards. Goldman Sachs, Morgan Stanley and other venerable investment banks have become bank holding companies.[21] This subjects the companies to far more government regulation, but provides access to government guarantees. In another example, Rolls-Royce plc has designed an innovative new aircraft engine which uses fuel more efficiently and, more importantly, can be scaled up or down, allowing the company to compete across a far wider range of aircraft than its competitors. In fact, Rolls-Royce is the only one of the three main engine-makers with designs to fit the three newest airliners, the Boeing 787 Dreamliner, the Airbus A380 and the new wide-bodied version of the Airbus A350.[22]

FIGURE 4 **CEOS ARE FOCUSED MOST ON RECONFIGURING THEIR BUSINESSES TO SPECIALIZE AND COLLABORATE**

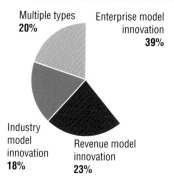

Multiple types
20%

Enterprise model innovation
39%

Industry model innovation
18%

Revenue model innovation
23%

Types of business model innovation considered

Industry model
Redefine an existing industry, move into a new industry or create an entirely new one.

Revenue model
Change how revenue is generated by introducing new pricing models.

Enterprise model
Reconfigure the business by rethinking what is done in-house and what is done through collaboration and partnering.

Source: *"The Enterprise of the Future: IBM Global CEO Study 2008." IBM Corporation.*

Identify and exploit new revenue models. New pricing models are emerging, particularly in digitized supply chains. In electronics, for example, the transition to a digital supply chain has substantially reduced inventories and thus the potential downward pressure on prices caused by oversupply. Indeed, the strength of supply chain management in this sector is expected to shorten the impact of the downturn. Other examples of digitized supply chains include Netflix for film, Apple's iTunes for music and Strayer for education.

Cultivate strategic partnerships. Partnering is a quick route to business model innovation. In today's environment, it's particularly important to differentiate between strategic partners and those offering more easily replaced commodity goods and services. With strategic partnerships, companies need a more collaborative approach, one aligned with the overall strategy and focused on the longer term. In the case of commodity-based relationships, now may be the time to drive down cost and look for alternatives. For those relationships that continue, a shared sense of engagement and interdependence, a tightening of collaboration, can help companies manage demand volatility and risk, and enable innovative new business models. For

> Discontinuity will likely bring about industry-changing business models.

example, Indian telecommunications leader Bharti Airtel has been able to grow quickly using a radical partnering strategy and business model.[23] Similarly, Lenovo was able to establish its full global presence much more quickly through its purchase of the IBM PC business than through organic growth.[24]

In another creative partnering strategy, companies such as Nintendo are using Web 2.0 approaches to engage customers in product development and customer service.[25]

ARE YOU READY?

- What is your company's competitive context (supply, demand, barriers to entry) and where do you fit?
- What new business models are likely to emerge in your industry? Are you working to get there ahead of your competitors?
- Are you watching other industries for concepts and business models that could transform your market?
- Do you have the right team – especially your top talent? Do they believe in your strategy to succeed?
- What capabilities do you need to develop to be ready for the upturn? Do you have a robust plan in place to develop them?
- If you had the cash, which companies and assets could you buy to change the game? Or could you be someone else's acquisition target?

ACT QUICKLY

Finally, the new environment will favor the fast and agile. Indeed, the urgency needed can provide a unique opportunity to overcome organizational inertia and barriers to strategic transformation. Transformation is never easy, but in the new economic environment it may be more possible than is usually the case.

1 Manage change

Overcome the "change gap." We learned in *The Enterprise of the Future* that eight out of ten CEOs anticipate substantial or very substantial change over the next three years, yet only six out of ten reported they had successfully managed change in the past, creating a "change gap" of 22 points.[26] Outperformers expect even more change but are significantly more adept at managing change than their peers. In a separate study entitled "Making Change Work" (see Chapter 3), we found that companies that are good at change management are really good at it.[27] On average, project practitioners rated only 41 percent of projects as successful. In contrast, the top 20 percent reported an 80 percent project success rate, nearly double the average, and they did this by following a systematic approach. They focused on:

- *Real insights for real actions* – striving for a full, realistic awareness, understanding the upcoming challenges and complexities, and taking actions to address them;
- *Solid methods for solid benefits* – using a systematic approach to change, one focused on outcomes and closely aligned with formal project management methods;
- *Better skills for better change* – demonstrating top management sponsorship, assigning dedicated change managers and empowering employees to enact change;
- *Right investment for the right impact* – allocating the right amount for change management by understanding which types of investments can offer the best returns in terms of greater project success.

2 Empower leaders

Establish strong and aligned leadership. In this environment, speed is of the essence, and strategy must be set from the top. Leadership teams must make decisive "no regrets" decisions and live with the consequences, correcting course as necessary. This is especially relevant for those cultures that are very consensus-oriented and find quick and decisive action difficult.

Communicate your strategy clearly and often. The challenge is to set an achievable strategy and manage change quickly and effectively. Doing this well requires the repeated communication of simple goals, together with clear targets and strong follow-through (including the measurement of results). It also requires the dedication and empowerment of high-ranking executives to act as change leaders, able to seek and leverage experience throughout their organizations and empower the layers beneath. It is essential that these leaders align around an agreed vision for the future and a course of action to achieve it.

3 Manage risk

Reduce risk and increase transparency. The issues of risk and transparency have come to the fore. To address these issues, organizations must apply analytics to improve decision-making and create greater predictive capability. They must also establish risk management governance and processes. And they must integrate and rationalize business information into the overall risk management process. Recent unprecedented losses in the financial services sector, as well as exposure to unseen threats of criminal activity such as the Madoff scheme, highlight the dangers of poor risk management and lack of transparency.[28] Our Global CFO Study confirmed that risk management is increasingly a boardroom issue, with each member of the executive team having a role and responsibility.[29]

Especially now, the ability to take requisite actions depends on having superior change management capabilities, strong leadership and robust risk management.

FIGURE 5 **THOSE WHO FOCUSED ON ALL FOUR FACETS OF WHAT WE CALL THE CHANGE DIAMOND EXPERIENCED AN OUTSTANDING INCREASE IN PROJECT SUCCESS**

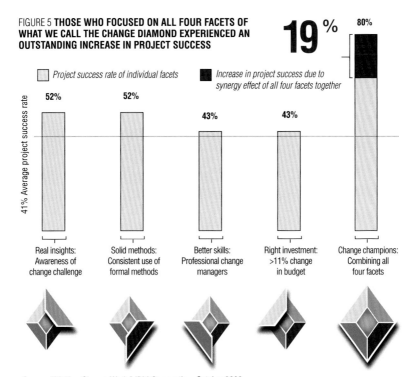

Source: "Making Change Work." IBM Corporation. October 2008.

ARE YOU READY?

- Does your organization have a consistent, tried and accepted method for change management?

- Does your organization invest in building change management skills that can be leveraged across projects?

- Are there processes and technologies in place that allow people to become involved in the change, to access accurate information and to provide feedback?

- Do your leaders share a common view of the future of the industries in which you operate? Of your own and your competitors' strengths and weaknesses? Do your leaders agree on where your organization needs to go?

- Do you understand the risks you are harboring? Do you know how vulnerable you are to changes in your operating environment?

- How transparent and timely is your management information? Are you tracking the variables that give you an accurate picture of the health of your company and the risks it faces?

CONCLUSION

To be sure, some companies will not survive these uncertain times. For the strong, however, the new economic environment may present rare, possibly once-in-a-lifetime opportunities. To seize them, companies must first establish financial stability in the short-term. But the winners will also invest for the medium and even the long term. As preconditions for success, companies will need:

- A robust understanding of how the transformation will affect their industries, as well as allied industries;
- A keen appreciation of their own core competencies and how these can be leveraged to take advantage of emerging opportunities and profitable innovation;
- Committed and aligned leadership with a clear strategy for creating sustainable competitive advantage so that the enterprise can move as swiftly as circumstances demand.

While the global financial crisis has unleashed a period of tremendous change and uncertainty, the good news is that even, and perhaps especially, in times like these, winners do emerge. And despite the noise, chaos and confusion, there are patterns in the strategies that winning companies use to navigate such times. Based on our experience, previous studies and an analysis of early winners in this period and longer-term winners from previous economic transformations, we advise business leaders to focus more sharply than ever on value, exploit opportunities presented by the new economic environment and act quickly in order to capitalize on these opportunities.

ABOUT THE AUTHORS

Saul Berman is a Partner and Global Executive of IBM Global Business Services and leads the IBM Global Strategy and Change practice. He has more than 25 years' experience consulting with senior management, has published extensively and is a frequent keynote speaker at major conferences. He was named one of the 25 most influential consultants of 2005 by *Consulting* magazine. He can be contacted at saul.berman@us.ibm.com.

Steven Davidson leads the IBM Strategy and Change consulting practice for growth markets, including Asia Pacific and Greater China. He also leads the IBM Institute for Business Value in Asia Pacific. Based in Hong Kong, he has 20 years of strategy consulting experience in Europe and Asia and works across industries to help clients develop and implement strategies and transformation programs in complex environments. He can be contacted at steven.davidson@hk1.ibm.com.

Sara Longworth leads the IBM Strategy and Change consulting practice in Europe, the Middle East and Africa. Based in London, she is particularly interested in the role of leadership in transformational change and has led engagements for European, American and Japanese multinationals to implement competitively advantageous operating models. She can be reached at saralongworth@uk.ibm.com.

Amy Blitz is a Director of Innovation Management Exchange. She has led major research initiatives on issues related to strategy, innovation and economic development. Her work has been featured in *Harvard Business Review* and *The Wall Street Journal* and at MSNBC and other major media outlets. She can be contacted at ablitz@alum.mit.edu.

CONTRIBUTORS

This paper would not have been possible without the substantial contributions of the IBM Strategy and Change team, notably Richard Christner, Dan Barter and Ragna Bell, who helped steer the content development; Dave Lubowe and Eric Riddleberger, who provided leadership and guidance throughout; Jim Byron for input on cost-reduction strategies; and Anubha Jain and Madhulika Kamjula for data analysis and overall research support.

REFERENCES

1   Much interesting research has explored patterns of economic transformation over long periods of time, from Nikolai Kondratiev to Joseph Schumpeter and more recently: Fernand Braudel's *Civilization and Capitalism, 15th-18th Century*, Berkeley: University of California Press, 1992; and Carlota Perez's *Technological Revolutions and Financial Capital: The Dynamics of Bubbles and Golden Ages*, Cheltenham, UK and Northampton, MA: E. Elgar Publishers, 2002. Perez, for example, argues that we are now in a period of transformation as the information revolution evolves from the "installation" to the "synergy" phase.

2   Fackler, Martin. "Toyota Expects Its First Loss in 70 Years." *The New York Times*. December 23, 2008. http://www.nytimes.com/2008/12/23/business/worldbusiness/23toyota.html

3   Perez, Carlota. Op. cit.

4   See Nelson, Scott Reynolds, "The Real Great Depression," *Chronicle Review,
    Chronicle of Higher Education,* October 17, 2008, Vol 55, Issue 8, for an
    interesting contrast between the 1930s and the 1870s, centering on the different
    sources of a severe downturn and the implications for economic recovery.

5   "Our Company: Under the Empire." Deutsche Bank. http://www.db.com/en/
    content/company/under_the_empire.htm

6   From IBM analysis of 2008 data of public companies listed on US exchanges.

7   We focused on public companies listed on AMEX, Nasdaq and the New York Stock
    Exchange with market capitalization greater than $US1.4 billion and whose stock
    appreciated by 5 percent or more in 2008, at a time when the S&P 500 Index
    declined by 37 percent. Our focus admittedly emphasizes US companies. We did
    this as a starting point because the crisis began in the US and so the impact and
    response registered most quickly there, providing more data for analysis at this
    point. The S&P performance data was accessed from: https://advisors.vanguard.
    com/VGApp/iip/site/advisor/investments/benchmarks/performanceSP?File=SPP
    erfReturns&bench=SP

8   "Rabobank Group Forecasts Moderate Growth in Profit in 2008." Rabobank
    Group press release. January 6, 2009. http://www.rabobank.com/content/news/
    news_archive/002-RabobankGroupforecastsmoderategrowthinprofitin2008.jsp

9   Strayer Education offers low-cost online degree programs at the undergraduate
    and graduate levels, primarily for working adults seeking professional
    advancement. Netflix Inc.'s relatively inexpensive DVD rental service delivers
    the majority of its selections to customers through the US Postal Service, but also
    offers a subset of titles that can be instantly streamed through high-speed Internet
    connections at no additional charge.

10 "An Interview with Satoshi Miura, President and CEO." http://www.ntt.co.jp/
    ir/library_e/nttis/2008aut/interview.html; "NEC Video Delivery Platform,
    'NC7500-VD,' Supported by NTT's NGN Business Services." NEC Corporation
    press release. November 6, 2008. http://www.nec.com.au/mediareleases08/
    ngnbusinessservices.htm

11 McGeehan, Patrick. "On Seventh Avenue, Goodbye, Lehman, Hello, Barclays." City
    Room Blog. *The New York Times.* September 24, 2008.

12 Whitehead, Jennifer. "Tesco's Discount Gamble." *Brand Republic News.*
    September 30, 2008.

13 Johnson, Kimberly, and Tom Krisher. "Ford Bailout Money Unnecessary, Company
    Says." Associated Press. December 10, 2008.

14 Ibid.

15 "Waitrose Grows Customer Numbers and is Britain's Top Grocer for Consumer
    Satisfaction." Waitrose press release. January 15, 2009. http://www.waitrose.
    presscentre.com/Content/Detail.aspx?ReleaseID=888&NewsAreaID=2

16 IBM Corporation. "Generating Higher Value at IBM." March 2009. http://www.
    ibm.com/annualreport/2008/

17 Scott, Mark. "Tesco Defies Gravity." *Der Spiegel.* April 16, 2008.

18 McGeehan, Patrick. Op. cit; Wai-yin Kwok, Vivian. "Nomura Wins the Lehman
    Asia Stakes." *Forbes.* September 22, 2008.

19 "Iceland Buys 51 Woolworths Stores." BBC News. January 9, 2009.

20 IBM Corporation. "IBM Archives: 1930s." http://www-03.ibm.com/ibm/history/
    history/decade_1930.html

21 Schroeder, Robert. "Goldman Sachs, Morgan Stanley to Become Bank Holding Companies." *MarketWatch*. September 21, 2008.

22 "Rolls-Royce: Britain's Lonely High-Flier." *The Economist*. January 8, 2009.

23 de Asis Martinez-Jerez, F., V. G. Narayanan and Michele Jurgens. "Strategic Outsourcing at Bharti Airtel Ltd." Harvard Business School Publishing. July 12, 2006.

24 "Lenovo Buys IBM PC for $US1.25b." Alibaba. August 19, 2008.

25 Porta, Matt, Brian House, Lisa Buckley and Amy Blitz. "Value 2.0: Eight new rules for creating and capturing value from innovative technologies." IBM Institute for Business Value. January 2008.

26 IBM Corporation. "The Enterprise of the Future: IBM Global CEO Study 2008." May 2008. http://www.ibm.com/enterpriseofthefuture. Based on availability of financial information, we were able to include 530 companies in our financial analysis. We compared performance on three financial benchmarks: revenue compound annual growth rate (CAGR) 2003-2006; net profit margin CAGR 2003-2006; and absolute profit margin average for 2003-2006. Companies that performed above the average for those in the same industry were tagged outperformers; those below the average were labeled underperformers.

27 Jørgensen, Hans Henrik, Lawrence Owen and Andreas Neus. "Making Change Work." IBM Corporation. October 2008.

28 Gandel, Stephen. "Wall Street's Latest Downfall: Madoff Charged with Fraud." *Time*. December 12, 2008.

29 Rogers, Stephen, Stephen Lukens, Spencer Lin and Edwina Jon. "Balancing Risk and Performance with an Integrated Finance Organization: The Global CFO Study 2008." IBM Corporation in co-operation with The Wharton School and Economist Intelligence Unit. October 2007.

Insights Succeeding in the new economic environment

More than 1,000 CEOs engaged with IBM in the discussions that underpin *The Enterprise of the Future*. In a series of follow-up video interviews conducted for the study by 50 Lessons, the world's premier multimedia business resource – and in interviews previously conducted by 50 Lessons – some of the world's top business leaders speak to the study's key themes.

Maurice Lévy, Chairman and CEO of Publicis Groupe, on reinventing the organization in tough times.

One of the problems we have as an ad agency is the fact that not only must we always deliver the best possible service to a client, always use the best tools available and create some of the best programs, but – as life is not easy – we also need to cope with some of the constraints of our business. So when there is a recession, we have to make sure that we can cope with it, and when there is a pick-up, that we don't have a huge rise in our cost.

The best way to do that is for us constantly to reinvent ourselves. In 1992 there was a very serious recession in France. Most – and when I say most, it was all – of our competitors had laid off something like 20 percent of their people. It was huge – 20 or 25 percent. There were companies or agencies that laid off much more – 300 people, which is huge for an ad agency, perhaps 40 percent of their staff.

And we thought, "These people are not responsible for this crisis; these people have created our wealth, and to lay them off just because there is a recession seems unfair to them." So we tried to create something. We created what we called "the economic revolution." This was a caucus over one month, every evening, where all the people in the agency met to try to find solutions. Then we came up with an idea: a referendum asking if everyone was ready to cut their salaries, starting with the CEO, in order to avoid the layoffs.

It worked. Not only did it work, but we'd thought it would be necessary to cut salaries for two years, [yet] after one year we were able to re-establish the original salaries. So you see that by being innovative in the way you manage the structure and change it, and manage your people, you can find the resource for more energy and more talent, and create a culture that is shared by the people. They feel good about the company, they feel good about the way we care, and obviously they work much more.

So never stabilize an organization; never think that the organization is forever. Always create an instability in the organization and make sure that you can move the borders – from one department to another, or one organization to another – very quickly. Be fast in creating the opportunity for reinventing yourself.

Maurice Lévy is the Chairman and CEO of Publicis Groupe, one of the world's largest advertising and media services conglomerates, with headquarters in Paris and offices in more than 100 countries. Publicis manages advertising and media services for such brands as Cadbury, Coca-Cola, General Mills and Procter & Gamble.

Anders Dahlvig, former Group President and CEO of IKEA, on a counter-intuitive downturn strategy.

In the year 2000, I was early in my career as the CEO of IKEA and the economy was at a peak. We were in the middle of the IT boom and IKEA was doing tremendously well. We had a sales growth pace of 15 percent to 20 percent. But something made me feel cautious about the economy. I believe my caution came from my time as a country manager in the mid-1990s during a downturn in the economy. We reacted to this downturn by reducing cost and laying off staff, and our customers reacted very negatively. So as I sat there in 2000 during an upturn in the economy, I decided that we needed to plan ahead. As we all know, after sunshine comes rain, but you can plan for this.

We set out to plan for the next downturn by running a series of scenarios. We looked at what the financial consequences would be if our turnover went down x percent, y percent or z percent and what actions we might take. As we continued to plan for the downturn, we looked at what the impact would be if we invested in the business. Our proposal was to increase our investments in new stores and to decrease prices. These represented a number of measures that most do not think about in a downturn.

We took the plan to the board, and we demonstrated the various scenarios and what our plan would be under each scenario. This gave us the opportunity to have a meaningful discussion at a time when the economy was good. We had time to comfortably discuss the scenarios in the meeting and come to a level of agreement.

Soon thereafter it happened – the IT bubble burst, and we had an IT crash. In 2002 and 2003, the entire Western economy went down dramatically. We embarked on our plan and did exactly as we had planned. We increased our store expansion from ten stores per year to 20 stores per year, reduced prices 2 percent to 3 percent, and increased our store hours to provide better service to our customers. In retrospect that was a very successful strategy because it put us significantly ahead of our competitors.

In planning for a downturn, you have to be prepared for the downturn to occur. You need to create plans and have the board and your management teams with you. This gave us the ability to be ahead of the competition and helped us to stay out of a reactionary mindset. The lesson is: Create an offensive strategy in a downturn and distance yourself from the competition.

Anders Dahlvig was the Group President and CEO of IKEA, a leading international retailer of home furnishing products, for 10 years until September 2009. IKEA offers more than 12,000 products and has 300 stores in 37 countries. From 1998 to 2008, sales grew from 6.3 billion euros to more than 21.2 billion euros.

These insights are drawn from interviews published by Harvard Business Press in Built for Change, *an exclusive edition of the Lessons Learned series and the result of a content partnership between IBM and 50 Lessons.*

Making change work

Closing the change gap

Hans Henrik Jørgensen,
Lawrence Owen and Andreas Neus

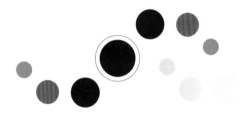

In the new economic environment, continuous change is becoming the new normal. To survive and succeed, the Enterprise of the Future must better anticipate and manage change. A detailed analysis of new data from our Making Change Work study shows that project success does not hinge primarily on technology – instead, it depends largely on people. But what is more illuminating is the discovery that four factors can help practitioners lead successful change by addressing their greatest project challenges. And when used in combination, these factors deliver more than the sum of their individual effects.

Today's dynamic work environment is causing organizations to reframe their view of "normal." Globalization, technology advances, multinational organizational complexity, more frequent partnering across national borders and company boundaries – these are just a few of the enablers and accelerators of change. No longer will companies have the luxury of expecting day-to-day operations to fall into a static or predictable pattern interrupted only occasionally by short bursts of change. To prosper, leaders will need to abandon such outdated notions of change. In reality, the new normal is continuous change – not the absence of change.

The IBM CEO Study 2008 identified five core traits of the Enterprise of the Future and found that outperforming companies are "hungry for change."[1] These organizations are capable of changing quickly and successfully. Instead of merely responding to trends, they shape and lead them. However, we also learned from the study that there is a change gap and it is growing.

The ability to manage change must be a core competence – and yet, as the level of expected change continues to rise, many are struggling to keep up. Eight out of ten CEOs anticipate substantial or very substantial change over the next three years, yet only six out of ten reported they had successfully managed change in the past – a "change gap" that has nearly tripled since 2006.[2] The widening gap stems from change that is more complex and more uncertain and occurring at an accelerated pace. CEOs are wrestling with a broader set of challenges than in the past, which introduces even greater risk and uncertainty.

Inability to close the change gap hurts the bottom line. Troubled projects typically create cost overruns while falling short of desired objectives related to time, budget and/or quality, as well as failing to deliver business value. The true cost of troubled projects is difficult to measure, but a European research study found that the low-end of such estimates cites an average cost amounting to 134 percent of the original plan – other estimates of the average cost of troubled projects were much higher.[3]

Bombarded by change on virtually all fronts, financially outperforming companies had a much smaller change gap than their peers in financially

FIGURE 1 **THE CHANGE GAP IS SMALLER FOR OUTPERFORMERS**

Because outperformers manage change well, they can get ahead of – and even be the drivers of – change.

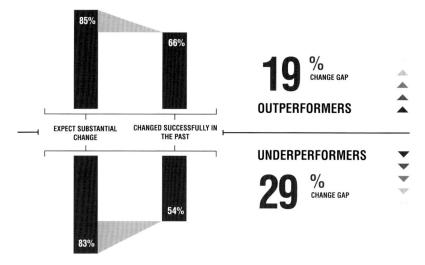

underperforming companies.[4] Notably, the outperformers did not face fewer challenges than others; they simply anticipated more change and were more effective at managing the change.

First we will highlight some of the most compelling study findings, including a deeper dive into the impact of change on organizations and the keys to successful change. Later, we will explore specific, practical actions that helped practitioners attain extraordinary results.

DEALING WITH CHANGE

Most CEOs consider themselves and their organizations to be executing change poorly, yet a few outperformers excel at delivering and benefiting from meaningful change. But how is this accomplished? What are the critical challenges? What factors can lead to change that succeeds?

FIGURE 2 **DEMOGRAPHICS: GLOBAL MAKING CHANGE WORK STUDY**

The Global Making Change Work 2008 Study covered organizations of all sizes, balanced around the globe and across industries. N = 1,532

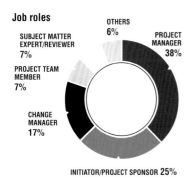

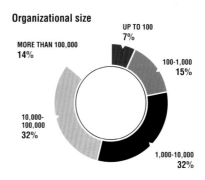

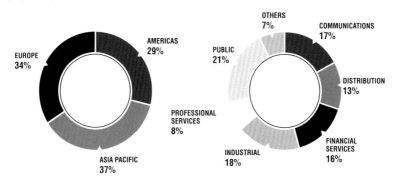

"Leaders are unrealistic about how change is going to happen. They move ahead anyway and get into problems."
Change Manager, UK, Energy and Utilities company

Based on new survey data from our Making Change Work study, this chapter continues the conversation from *The Enterprise of the Future* and describes the practical steps organizations must take to better prepare for an unrelenting barrage of change. We looked more closely at the Enterprise of the Future trait "Hungry for Change" and we engaged 1,532 key practitioners through surveys and face-to-face interviews, revealing many useful insights based on their real-world experiences (see Figure 2).

These project leaders were responsible for small- and large-scale efforts intended to execute strategic, organizational, operational and technology-based change. The diverse range of projects had objectives that included customer satisfaction improvement, sales and revenue growth, cost reduction, process innovation, technology implementation, new market entry and organizational change. The Center for Evaluation and Methods (ZEM) at the University of Bonn, Germany, aggregated the data and provided statistical support for analysis of the results.

Project leaders confirmed that project success is indeed hard to come by. In our study, we learned that only 41 percent of projects were considered successful in meeting project objectives within planned time, budget and quality constraints. Nearly 60 percent of projects failed to fully meet their objectives; 44 percent missed at least one time, budget or quality goal; and a full 15 percent either missed all goals or were stopped by management (see Figure 3).

FIGURE 3 **PROJECT SUCCESS RATES: PROJECT LEADERS REPORTED THAT 41 PERCENT OF PROJECTS WERE CONSIDERED SUCCESSFUL**

Forty-four percent of all projects failed to meet either time, budget or quality goals, while 15 percent either stop or fail to meet all objectives.

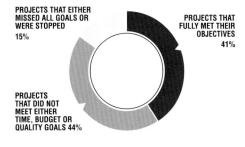

PROJECTS THAT EITHER MISSED ALL GOALS OR WERE STOPPED 15%

PROJECTS THAT FULLY MET THEIR OBJECTIVES 41%

PROJECTS THAT DID NOT MEET EITHER TIME, BUDGET OR QUALITY GOALS 44%

On average, practitioners rated only 41 percent of projects as successful, defined as meeting time, budget and quality goals. Yet the top 20 percent of our sample – we call them "change masters" – reported an 80 percent project success rate. In sharp contrast, we describe the bottom 20 percent of our sample as "change novices" – their reported project success rate was a dismal 8 percent. Their low success rate reflects the difficulty of getting all project factors to work as planned – just one broken link in the chain can lead to project failure (see Figure 4).

Troubled or failed projects create cost overruns and, by definition, fall short of achieving the desired objectives. When nearly 60 percent of projects fail to meet objectives, significant expense is incurred in terms of wasted money, lost opportunity and lack of focus. Change masters understand that reducing the likelihood of troubled projects, even slightly, can have a clear and rapid payback.

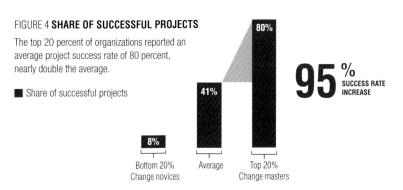

FIGURE 4 **SHARE OF SUCCESSFUL PROJECTS**

The top 20 percent of organizations reported an average project success rate of 80 percent, nearly double the average.

■ Share of successful projects

80%

41%

8%

Bottom 20%
Change novices

Average

Top 20%
Change masters

95 **% SUCCESS RATE INCREASE**

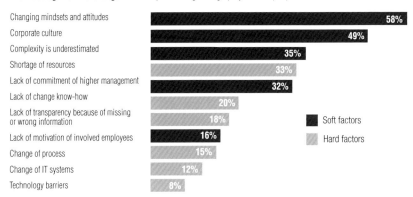

FIGURE 5 **MAJOR CHANGE CHALLENGES**

The most significant challenges when implementing change projects are people-oriented.

Changing mindsets and attitudes	58%
Corporate culture	49%
Complexity is underestimated	35%
Shortage of resources	33%
Lack of commitment of higher management	32%
Lack of change know-how	20%
Lack of transparency because of missing or wrong information	18%
Lack of motivation of involved employees	16%
Change of process	15%
Change of IT systems	12%
Technology barriers	8%

■ Soft factors
▨ Hard factors

Our respondents identified several of the key barriers to change. Although tangible tasks such as change of IT systems or addressing technology barriers may be expected to present difficulties, our practitioners did not report them among their greatest challenges. Instead, the main obstacles they identified were changing mindsets and attitudes (58 percent), corporate culture (49 percent) and underestimating project complexity (35 percent). Project professionals – who typically request more time, more people and more money – reported that these soft challenges are more problematic than shortage of resources.

Surprisingly, it turns out the "soft stuff" is the hardest to get right. Changing mindsets, attitudes and culture in an organization typically require different techniques, applied consistently and over time – sometimes across a series of successive projects and often continuing after the formal "project" has finished. Practitioners typically find such less concrete challenges tougher to manage and measure than those related to business processes or technology, which are more tangible and may possibly be changed permanently through a single intervention.

The list of greatest project challenges was top-heavy with soft factors. When asked to identify key factors for successful change, practitioners repeated the difficulty in dealing with less tangible aspects of a project. Practitioners firmly place key responsibility for the fate of change projects in the executive suite – an overwhelming 92 percent named top management sponsorship as the most important factor for successful change. Rounding out the top four success factors were employee involvement (72 percent), honest and timely communication (70 percent) and a corporate culture that motivates and promotes change (65 percent).

In fact, the top six answers all referenced "soft" aspects of change, ranking them above efficient organization structure and above monetary and non-monetary incentives. Change masters have realized that behavioral and cultural change are crucial to project success and are considerably tougher to address than the so-called "hard" factors, such as structure, performance measures and incentives.

FIGURE 6 **WHAT MAKES CHANGE SUCCESSFUL?**
Leadership, employee engagement and honest communication are prerequisites for successful change.

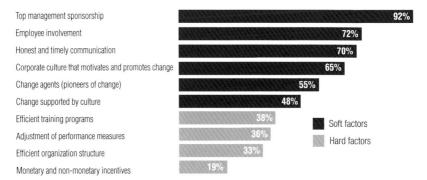

Top management sponsorship	92%
Employee involvement	72%
Honest and timely communication	70%
Corporate culture that motivates and promotes change	65%
Change agents (pioneers of change)	55%
Change supported by culture	48%
Efficient training programs	38%
Adjustment of performance measures	36%
Efficient organization structure	33%
Monetary and non-monetary incentives	19%

■ Soft factors
▨ Hard factors

THE CHANGE MASTERS

We have seen that organizations differ greatly in rates of project success, but why? Detailed analysis of our study results revealed a highly significant correlation between project success and four important areas of focus: real insights; solid methods; better skills; and right investment.

These four change-related focus areas are represented graphically as four facets of what we call the Change Diamond. When combined effectively, taking actions to address each of the diamond's four facets can help guide the Enterprise of the Future in its quest to make change work:

"Culture isn't just one aspect of the game, it is the game."
Lou Gerstner, former IBM CEO

Real insights, real actions: Strive for a full, realistic understanding of the coming challenges and complexities, then follow with actions to address them.

Solid methods, solid benefits: Use a systematic approach to change that is focused on outcomes and closely aligned with formal project management methodology.

Better skills, better change: Leverage resources appropriately to demonstrate top management sponsorship, assign dedicated change managers and empower employees to enact change.

Right investment, right impact: Allocate the right amount for change management through understanding which forms of investments can offer the best returns, in terms of greater project success.

FIGURE 7 **THE CHANGE DIAMOND**
By focusing on the four facets of the change diamond, practitioners achieved significantly higher rates of project success.

RIGHT INVESTMENT
RIGHT IMPACT

REAL INSIGHTS
REAL ACTIONS

BETTER SKILLS
BETTER CHANGE

SOLID METHODS
SOLID BENEFITS

REAL INSIGHTS, REAL ACTIONS

Successful projects require a full, realistic understanding of the challenges and complexities, followed by specific actions to address them. Lack of early insight leads to a high risk that complexity will be underestimated or even overlooked. In particular, the complexity of behavioral and cultural changes is often underestimated in the early project planning and scoping stages.

When asked if there was sufficient awareness of the challenges associated with implementing and sustaining change, practitioners replying "yes" reported a 52 percent project success rate within their organizations. Project success rates dropped as organizations' awareness levels decreased, down to a low 25 percent success rate for those practitioners who answered "no" to the question.

But awareness of complexity alone is not enough – action is the vital next step. Only 18 percent of project leaders in our study reported that their organi-

FIGURE 8 **WE FOUND A STRONG CORRELATION BETWEEN SUCCESSFUL PROJECTS AND A REALISTIC AWARENESS OF THE CHANGE CHALLENGE**
Responses to the question: "Within your organization, do you think there is sufficient awareness of the challenges associated with implementing and sustaining change?"

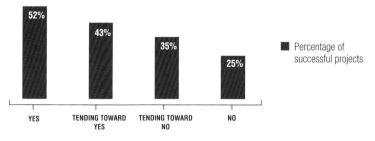

52%
43%
35%
25%

■ Percentage of successful projects

YES | TENDING TOWARD YES | TENDING TOWARD NO | NO

zations had sufficient awareness of the challenges associated with implementing and sustaining change. But of that small group, 95 percent said that their awareness led to the introduction of specific measures to support change.

FIGURE 9 **BEING MERELY AWARE OF CHANGE COMPLEXITY IS INSUFFICIENT**

Action as a result of awareness is critical to more successful change efforts.

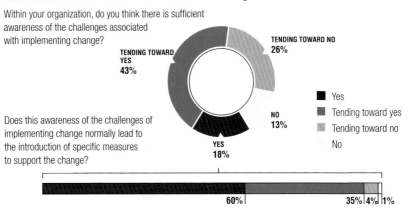

Within your organization, do you think there is sufficient awareness of the challenges associated with implementing change?

TENDING TOWARD YES
43%

TENDING TOWARD NO
26%

Does this awareness of the challenges of implementing change normally lead to the introduction of specific measures to support the change?

NO
13%

YES
18%

- Yes
- Tending toward yes
- Tending toward no
- No

60% 35% 4% 1%

Early awareness and actions are critical to address the top organizational challenges inherent in change projects shown earlier: mindsets, attitudes, culture and complexity. Such changes do not happen automatically – the change masters address them early, plan carefully and execute rigorously. Changing an organization requires complex change simultaneously at many levels – and organizations tend to build a kind of "immune system" to fend off disruptive influences. Early awareness and consequent action help to address the natural response of an organization to resist attempts to change it. Some practical steps include:

Hook into the history: Provide change leaders with access to historical data, people surveys, culture assessments and "war stories," as well as the people involved in previous projects, if possible. Learn from both good and bad experiences and be especially vigilant in seeking insights into the soft aspects of the organization undergoing change.

Open your eyes ... wide: Examine the project's scope, likely impacts and expected outcomes carefully. Assess the dimensions of the change – people, culture, behavior and organizational aspects, as well as process and technology impacts. Be realistic in defining the necessary change and communicate that information widely within the organization.

Plan and adjust: With a thorough understanding of project complexities, build a change plan to address them. As the plan is communicated, tested and executed, be prepared to adapt it frequently as needed to handle the unexpected.

Take a long view: Be prepared to build and execute plans to address the "soft stuff" well beyond the formal end date of the project to deliver business value. Changing these aspects takes time, patience as well as consistent and continuous activity. Be prepared to continue these activities beyond project boundaries deeper into the organization.

SOLID METHODS, SOLID BENEFITS

For most organizations, classic project management, with its formal and structured elements, has been used for decades. But formal change management methods have not yet permeated business or project operations to a significant degree. Today's change management, if explicitly performed at all, often occurs in the form of improvised solutions.

But a consistent and structured change management approach yielded tangible benefits for companies in our study. Practitioners who always follow specific and formal change management procedures had a 52 percent project success rate, compared with a 36 percent success rate for practitioners who improvise according to the situation. It is interesting to note that even those who had a formal method – but did not use it consistently – fared slightly better than those who improvised (39 percent, versus 38 and 36 percent).

FIGURE 10 **FORMAL CHANGE MANAGEMENT METHODS CAN ONLY IMPROVE PROJECT SUCCESS IF THEY ARE APPLIED**

Project success rates were best for organizations that consistently used structured change management methods – a variety of less formal approaches all resulted in success rates below average (41 percent).

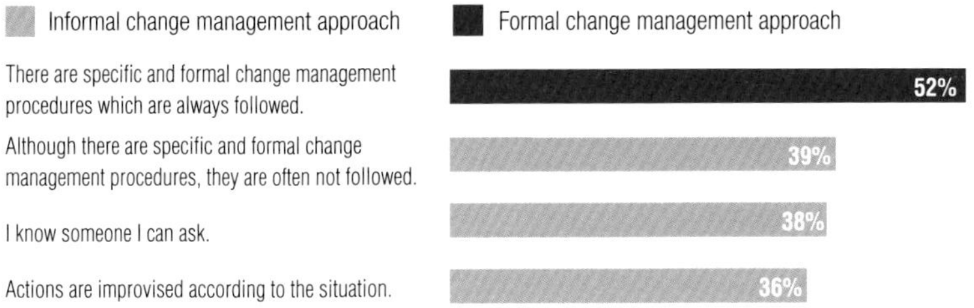

Informal change management approach   Formal change management approach

There are specific and formal change management procedures which are always followed. **52%**

Although there are specific and formal change management procedures, they are often not followed. **39%**

I know someone I can ask. **38%**

Actions are improvised according to the situation. **36%**

Only 24 percent of practitioners in our study consistently used formal change management methods. Seventy-six percent said their approach to change management was usually informal (25 percent), ad hoc (8 percent) or improvised (43 percent). In contrast, just over half of our respondents applied formal project management procedures consistently.

Overwhelmingly, the change management approaches of project leaders are quite immature. As organizations face increases in both the absolute volume of change and its level of complexity, widespread improvisation must yield to professional, formal change management methods – a priority most are beginning to recognize.

When asked whether standard change management approaches were necessary, 87 percent of practitioners answered either "yes" or tending toward "yes." This contrast – between those seeing the value of standard methods and those actually

FIGURE 11 **CHANGE MANAGEMENT METHODS ARE USUALLY INFORMAL, AD HOC OR IMPROVISED**

Seventy-six percent of organizations use a change management approach that is typically informal, ad hoc or improvised; by contrast, 49 percent of organizations failed to use formal project management methods consistently.

■ Formal methods are used consistently
☐ Formal methods exist but not used on a consistent basis, ad hoc or improvised

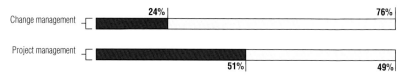

using them – indicates that the need for change is outpacing organizations' capability to manage it systematically. In essence, it is a "methods gap."

Growing project complexity and increased sensitivity regarding the "softer" or hidden dimensions of change is accelerating the establishment of formal change management in the project mainstream and its integration into project management. Change management is transforming gradually from an art to a profession, similar to the evolution of the project management discipline, which has undergone a formalization that started about four decades ago.

FIGURE 12 **THE METHODS GAP**

Despite the overwhelming majority of project leaders who recognize the value in standardizing change management practices, very few consistently use a systematic approach.

■ Percent answering "yes"

Putting solid methods into practice begins with allocating resources to enact a change method that is aligned with the organization's project management approach. Then it must be used consistently across the organization. Developing a standard change methodology should include these practical steps:

Integrate, integrate, integrate: Manage change as a formal workstream within each and every project, integrated closely with project management and managed with the same rigor.

Keep all eyes on the prize: Control the scope of the change effort to remain focused on activities that drive the realization of benefits defined by the original business case.

Drive consistency: Develop and promote a standard change method that can be applied consistently from project to project within your organization. Communicate this widely and monitor its adoption.

Embed in the culture: Include the change method and associated competencies as part of the development program for future leaders.

BETTER SKILLS, BETTER CHANGE

Using more experienced and skilled change managers and project sponsors can mean reduced risk of troubled projects. Effective change leadership in the form of dedicated change managers and credible and experienced sponsors is critical. It is equally important to cascade leadership responsibility to all levels of the organization, creating empowered employees who support and enact change.

FIGURE 13 **SHARE OF SUCCESSFUL PROJECTS, INVOLVEMENT OF CHANGE MANAGERS**
Success rates rose when a change manager was used on a project.

■ Share of successful projects

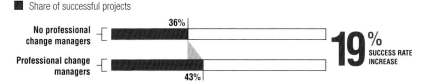

No professional change managers 36%
Professional change managers 43%

19% SUCCESS RATE INCREASE

Practitioners found that dedicating a change manager to a project increased the likelihood of project success. Yet 20 percent of change projects did not involve a change manager at all. Projects with a professional change manager had a 43 percent success rate, compared with a 36 percent success rate for projects without one.

Our findings showed that practitioners consider top management sponsorship to be the most critical factor for making change successful. To improve strategy execution, leaders need to engage, enable and empower employees at all levels of the organization.[5] Top sponsorship is equally vital in other areas, such as setting corporate culture and allocating resources, including the change managers themselves.

> "Facilitate involvement of employees and allow them to exercise influence over the change process."
> *Project Sponsor, Canada, Life Sciences and Pharmaceuticals*

Our findings suggest the need for broader inclusion of people at different levels in the organization. Besides the familiar top-down hierarchy that formally cascades unit-specific information, change masters see the value in and make use of informal, more self-organized communications structures, such as social networks, "the grapevine" and the informal communities of interest that exist in all organizations.

Engaging employees through involvement and two-way communication is a powerful combination: 72 percent of practitioners believe employee involvement is crucial and 70 percent believe honest and timely communication is important. Better communications and employee involvement enable and empower people, and then change happens through them – not just to them.

Change leaders with participative leadership styles were more likely to have successful projects. A strong culture of empowerment and delegation of decision-making power distributes responsibility for change throughout the organization.

FIGURE 14 **SHARE OF SUCCESSFUL PROJECTS, A COMPARISON OF LEADERSHIP STYLES**
Leadership styles had an important impact on project outcomes..

■ Share of successful projects

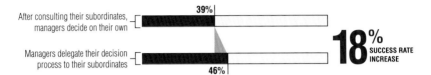

Leaders who delegate the decision process to their subordinates had a 46 percent project success rate, compared with a 39 percent success rate for those who consult with subordinates, then make decisions on their own.

For teams involved in change, enabling skills and engagement across the organization should be a key priority to help build the capabilities to support continuous change. Some practical suggestions include:

Lead from the top: Set vision and direction clearly, allocating resources and establishing corporate culture from the top. A change sponsor should be actively and visibly involved in setting overall direction, publicly communicating at all levels and using different techniques and media, and dedicating the right skilled resources to the change effort.

Involve the people: Emphasize employee involvement to ease resistance to change, at both individual and group levels, and set in place mechanisms to encourage this involvement.

Communicate or fail: Enable honest and timely two-way communication to build trust and commitment to change programs and leaders, and reduce resistance. Use multiple channels and different media. Take time to understand the audience and how it likes to communicate.

Get the right skills – everywhere: Enable rapid development of internal skills to keep pace with changes in the external environment. Consider the establishment of a sustainable change management capability within the organization.

RIGHT INVESTMENT, RIGHT IMPACT

The right budget for change management, spent effectively on the right things translated into a significantly higher likelihood of project success. However, depending upon the objectives of a particular project, the "right" level of investment in change management will vary. Reinforcing the anticipated value from such investments, a massive 72 percent of project leaders would like to invest more in change management for future projects.

In fact, top organizations invested only 18 percent more in change than others, but were rewarded with significantly higher project success. This incremental amount was typically used to focus on developing insights, methods and the right skills to be truly effective. Project success rates were 23 percent higher when the amount invested in change was greater than 11 percent of the project budget.

Making more effective investments in change is not about blindly diverting unlimited sums of money into projects. Rather, it is about cutting the diamond precisely, through focused investments in the right things for each specific situation.

Organizations need the right budget to build strategic capabilities and integrate them into organizational processes and structures – investing just a little more than average per project can greatly improve results. Change masters consider money spent on change management as an investment, rather than an expenditure. Some practical ideas include:

FIGURE 15 THE MAJORITY OF PROJECT LEADERS WOULD LIKE TO INVEST MORE TO CLOSE THE CHANGE GAP

Comparing current investments to plans for future projects.

Compared to current investment in change management, on future projects would you ...

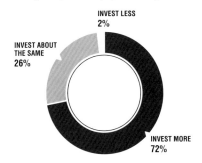

INVEST LESS
2%

INVEST ABOUT
THE SAME
26%

INVEST MORE
72%

Tackle complexity before it tackles you: Invest upfront in gaining and acting upon insights that can help you avoid and overcome both expected and unexpected hurdles during the course of a project.

Remember to emphasize the human touch: Invest in skills by using well-trained change managers more consistently and enable widespread communications that engage employees across all organizational levels.

Put some method into your madness: Invest in establishing standardized methods to build more effective and long-term capabilities that support change efforts, and remain vigilant about project spending overall.

FIGURE 16 INVESTMENT LEVELS

Organizations that invested less than 11 percent in change had a 35 percent success rate; those that invested more than 11 percent had a 43 percent success rate.

■ Share of successful projects

Investment <=11%   35%

Investment >11%   43%

23%
SUCCESS RATE
INCREASE

SECRETS FOR SUCCESS: THE CHANGE DIAMOND

Our search for the key to greater project success brings us back to the change masters, who achieved success rates nearly double the average. We discovered that change masters did not limit their focus to just one facet of the Change Diamond. Instead, this group took actions related to each of the four facets of the Change Diamond – and project success improved substantially as a result. Conversely, change novices underutilized every facet and had far inferior results, even when compared to just the average.

While each Change Diamond facet had a distinct benefit individually, when companies combined all four facets their overall project success increased dramatically – far more than the sum of the parts would indicate. Neglecting even one area can inhibit change excellence. By combining all four facets, change masters attained an 80 percent success rate – an increase far beyond the sum of the individual effects (see Figures 17 and 18).

FIGURE 17 **HOW CHANGE MASTERS AND CHANGE NOVICES UTILIZED OR UNDERUTILIZED EACH FACET**

High concentration on all facets of the Change Diamond correlated to significantly higher project success rates.

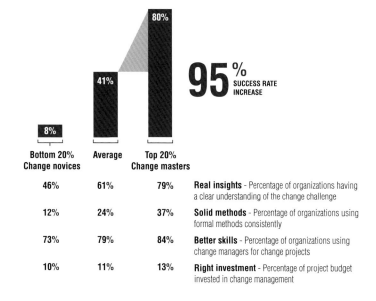

Bottom 20% Change novices	Average	Top 20% Change masters	
46%	61%	79%	**Real insights** - Percentage of organizations having a clear understanding of the change challenge
12%	24%	37%	**Solid methods** - Percentage of organizations using formal methods consistently
73%	79%	84%	**Better skills** - Percentage of organizations using change managers for change projects
10%	11%	13%	**Right investment** - Percentage of project budget invested in change management

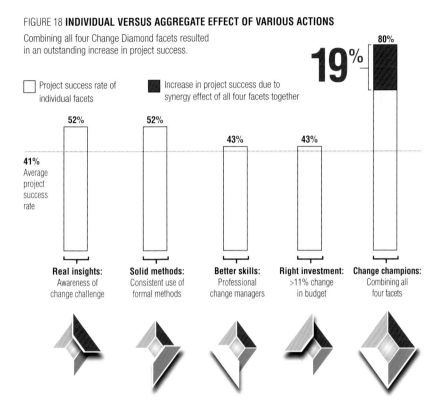

FIGURE 18 **INDIVIDUAL VERSUS AGGREGATE EFFECT OF VARIOUS ACTIONS**

Combining all four Change Diamond facets resulted in an outstanding increase in project success.

☐ Project success rate of individual facets

◼ Increase in project success due to synergy effect of all four facets together

19% 80%

52% 52% 43% 43%

41% Average project success rate

Real insights: Awareness of change challenge

Solid methods: Consistent use of formal methods

Better skills: Professional change managers

Right investment: >11% change in budget

Change champions: Combining all four facets

CONCLUSION

While the Enterprise of the Future is indeed hungry for change, our Making Change Work study shows that executing change well remains the exception, though it is certainly an achievable goal. Our research with practitioners revealed practical insights about closing the "change gap" – including the insight that soft, people-related factors typically present greater challenges than hard, technology-related factors, which are usually easier to identify and measure.

Companies can no longer justify or afford an ad hoc approach to change management. Change management is at a turning point from an art to a professional discussion, from improvisation to a richer, more systematic approach, based on clear empirical perspectives on what works and what does not.

Improving project outcomes requires attention to a combination of acting on real insights, employing better skills, establishing solid methods and allocating the right investments. By focusing on all four facets of the Change Diamond, organizations can achieve synergies that make change work in their favor, delivering more successful projects and building the change management capability that is vital to becoming an Enterprise of the Future.

ARE YOU READY?

Ask yourself the questions below. Your checkmarks can help you identify your strengths and weaknesses regarding each of the four facets of the Change Diamond. The resulting pattern can help your organization pinpoint where to take actions in order to learn how to better deal with change and reap the benefits of handling it well.

FIGURE 19 **HOW DO YOU RANK ON THE CHANGE DIAMOND FACETS**

Look for patterns in your answers to see where your organization most needs to improve.

	YES	TENDING TOWARD YES	TENDING TOWARD NO	NO
GAINING REAL INSIGHTS AND TURNING THEM INTO ACTIONS				
Does your organization have a good common understanding of why projects have failed or succeeded in the past?				
Are the people and cultural aspects of the change plan given emphasis equal to that placed on process and technological changes?				
Is change viewed as a long-term transformation that's part of a strategy, as opposed being seen as a succession of separate projects?				
MAKING GOOD USE OF METHODS				
Does your organization have a consistent, tried and accepted method for change management that is applied to every project?				
Do all projects have an approved business case, and a method for identifying and tracking benefits against that case?				
Is change managed as a formal workstream in all significant projects?				
LEVERAGING SKILLS FOR BETTER CHANGE				
Does your organization invest in building change management skills that can be leveraged across projects?				
Is the role of a project sponsor well defined, and is that role held accountable for specific communication and direction setting tasks?				
Are there processes and technologies in place to allow people to become involved in the change, get accurate information and provide feedback?				
INVESTING WISELY IN CHANGE MANAGEMENT				
Does your organization include change as a line item when budgeting projects?				
Is your change management budget set relative to project complexity and risk, as opposed to a straight percentage?				
Is the change budget focused largely on understanding and reacting to complexity, developing consistent methods and acquiring the best change skills?				

ABOUT THE AUTHORS

Hans Henrik Jørgensen is an Associate Partner in IBM Global Business Services and Global Lead of the Change Management Community. He has led numerous projects in the area of management and strategy consulting in Europe, the Americas and Asia over the past 15 years. He can be reached at hans-henrik.jorgensen@de.ibm.com.

Lawrence Owen is the Global Leader of the Organization and Change Strategy Practice within IBM Global Business Services. He is responsible for leading the development of organizational and change strategies with which clients can drive their transformation agendas, and manages one of the largest organization and change consulting teams globally. He can be reached at owenl@us.ibm.com.

Andreas Neus is a Senior Managing Consultant with the Strategy and Change practice of IBM Global Business Services and leads the service innovation research at the Karlsruhe Service Research Institute, founded jointly by Karlsruhe University and IBM. He can be reached at andreas.neus@de.ibm.com.

CONTRIBUTORS

Saul Berman, Global and Americas Strategy and Change Leader, IBM Global Services.

Peter Korsten, Global Leader of the IBM Institute for Business Value, IBM Global Services.

Mark Buckingham, Senior Managing Consultant, Strategy and Change, IBM Global Business Services.

Mike Ash, Senior Managing Consultant, Strategy and Change, IBM Global Business Services.

Jason Seng, Senior Consultant, Strategy and Change, IBM Global Business Services.

Jacqui Warren, Partner, Organization Change Strategy, UK and Ireland, IBM Global Business Services.

Georg Rudinger, Director, Centre for Evaluation and Methods (Zentrum für Evaluation und Methoden – ZEM), University of Bonn.

Sandra Pietrangeli, Project Manager, Centre for Evaluation and Methods, University of Bonn.

ACKNOWLEDGMENTS

True collaborative innovation was exhibited by more than 1,500 clients and many other colleagues throughout IBM who contributed to this paper. In particular, this paper benefited from additional input and research from Jörg Albrecht, Anna Bisch, Carolyn Burgemeister, Edwin de Groot, Rosane Giovis, Lars Gottschling-Knudsen, Daniela Humpert, Christoph Kaftan, Toru Kaneko, Patrick Kramer, Eunice Kwon, Jan Neumann, Si Young Park, Gaelle Pujo, Ayodele Sebilleau, Nathalie Svaiter, Grace To, Ray Wang and Shi Rong Zhang.

REFERENCES

1   IBM Corporation. "The Enterprise of the Future: IBM Global CEO Study 2008." May 2008. http://www.ibm.com/enterpriseofthefuture

2   Ibid.

3   Jørgensen, M. and K.J. Moløkken-Østvold. "How Large Are Software Cost Overruns? Critical Comments on the Standish Group's CHAOS Reports." *Information and Software Technology*. Vol 48 No 4. April 2006. http://simula. no/research/engineering/publications/Jorgensen.2006.4

4   Based on revenue compound annual growth rate for 2003-2006. IBM Corporation. Op. cit.

5   The findings from this study align with the academic literature. See for example: Kotter, John. "Leading Change: Why Transformation Efforts Fail." *Harvard Business Review*. March-April 1995.

Insights **Making change work**

More than 1,000 CEOs engaged with IBM in the discussions that underpin *The Enterprise of the Future*. In a series of follow-up video interviews conducted for the study by 50 Lessons, the world's premier multimedia business resource – and in interviews previously conducted by 50 Lessons – some of the world's top business leaders speak to the study's key themes.

William K. Fung, Group Managing Director of Li & Fung Limited, on institutionalizing the process of reinvention.

Our attitude about change is that change is inevitable. Not only is change inevitable, but it is happening faster and faster. Li & Fung has a very specific way of dealing with the management of change. First, most companies have planning cycles of three, five or even ten years. We decided that our planning cycles should be kept relatively short. Given the way the world is changing, even five-year plans are probably too long. And certainly no one is able to predict with any certainty what is going to happen in ten years' time. So Li & Fung sticks with a three-year plan.

The second aspect of planning is that most business schools will teach you something called the rolling plan. In other words, every year – whether within a three- or five-year plan – you redo the plan. At Li & Fung we think that approach moves the goalposts too much. We believe that if every year the plan changes, then no one will actually pay attention to the plan. We learned something from the Chinese Communist central planning system. They have five-year plans that are fixed. Li & Fung adapted and adopted that concept to three-year fixed plans. Within that three-year timeframe, most of our seasoned executives can actually foresee the changes coming down the pike with some certainty, or at least with enough certainty to plan properly in a three-year time horizon compared with a five- or a ten-year time horizon.

> "If you cannot look to the future and see the changes that are coming, then your company will not survive."

The next thing we do is look at the planning horizon from a zero base. To start planning from a zero base means that we ask ourselves whether we would be in our business today if we had a choice. Most companies just assume that they have to continue in their business; they don't stop to think about whether that is the business they would choose given their knowledge of the market. We ask ourselves this question every three years. The reason we do so comes from a philosophy held by my brother Victor. He believes that if you cannot look to the future and see the changes that are coming, then your company will not survive.

At Li & Fung we want to institutionalize the process of reinvention. The way we do that is through our three-year planning cycle. This forces people to think and plan systematically. We really spend the time and evaluate for the next three years the changes we foresee collectively as a team. Not only that, but we engage forecasting experts who are visionary and can see the types of changes that are coming. We have agreed to do this as a formal exercise every three years, and this is how we have institutionalized the process of reinvention.

William K. Fung is the Group Managing Director of Li & Fung Limited, one of the largest supply chain management companies. Li & Fung, which is based in Hong Kong, is forecasting turnover of $US20 billion for 2008-10 and a core operating profit of $US1 billion by 2010. Mr Fung is also a Director of various companies within the Li & Fung group of companies, including publicly listed Convenience Retail Asia Limited and Integrated Distribution Services Group Limited.

Ravi Kant, Executive Vice-Chairman and former Managing Director of Tata Motors, on creating a culture of change.

People are used to looking at things in a certain manner. If they are required to change, it takes a long time. They say, "I have been successful doing this thing this way; therefore, I would not like to change." There is a resistance to change, especially with people who have been in the organization a long time. If you want to bring about change, there are three things you need to do. Number one is: Expose these people more and more to external environments. Force them to see that the world outside has changed and that they also have to change.

Number two is: Get people from outside the organization who have been through the change. You don't need many people, but a few people. You place them in the organization so that they begin to create that environment or activity of change and look at things in a different manner.

"If you want to bring about change, you need to ... expose people more and more to external environments ... get people from outside the organization ... pick younger people."

The third thing is: Pick younger people, people who are not so rooted in the previous philosophy or mindset. Ask them to take up challenges and do things in a somewhat different manner. It's a combination of these things. Not one of them taken alone is going to be successful. In Tata Motors, we have done all three.

We wanted to create a small truck. If I went through the normal routine, there would be problems. We picked out a young, bright, articulate person who could move around in the organization and get things done, and who was committed to delivery. He was in his early 30s. We gave him the opportunity. We built a team around him. He was supported by everybody in the organization, and he and his team went on to create what we call the small truck, the Ace, which has become a phenomenal success. This person, after the success of Ace, has been made project manager for Nano, our small car. He has gone from one success to hopefully another big success. Looking at that success, more and more people want newer and more challenging responsibilities. That's a big change.

Ravi Kant is Executive Vice-Chairman and former Managing Director of Tata Motors, India's largest automobile company. In 2007 Tata finalized an agreement to purchase the Jaguar and Land Rover brands from Ford for a reported $US2.3 billion, and in 2008 it unveiled the world's cheapest car, the Nano.

Manoj Kohli, Chief Executive Officer and Managing Director of Bharti Airtel, on how to encourage an entrepreneurial spirit.
This company is about change. Bharti Airtel, when it was launched in 1995, started with an entrepreneurial spirit, which is very important for any new company. We also started with a lot of passion and enthusiasm for success among our employees. The culture we built, and the DNA we built, was very change-oriented. We believed that you should love to change, that you should embrace change, that you should not worry about the side-effects of change. If you change faster, you'll be able to get on top of the market and your competitors. Luckily for us, our competition was slow. They were large companies; they were bureaucratic, hierarchic and not eager to change. Change, and the speed of change, became the biggest weapon of Bharti Airtel.

Let me come to the second stage, in 2005, when we initiated a new vision – to be the most admired brand by 2010. We adopted a new slogan: "Think fresh, deliver more." We said that, as a company, we want to think fresh every day. We want to think about new solutions to old problems, new solutions to new problems, paradigm shifts and things that are risky. Make mistakes, but don't repeat mistakes. The day you find out that there's a mistake, cut the cost on that day. We encourage making mistakes. We encourage taking risks.

Our culture was started as an entrepreneurial-entrepreneurial culture. That's good for a start, but it's not a sustainable culture. Then we changed it to an entrepreneurial-professional culture, where an entrepreneur leads it and professionals follow. This was important, because we had to build a large company. Now we are at the third stage, which is a professional-entrepreneurial culture, where professionals are leading and professionals themselves are entrepreneurs building the future.

The fourth stage is professional-professional, which you don't want to go to, because all the large multinationals are at that stage, where they have lost the entrepreneurial edge of the company. We'll stay as a professional-entrepreneurial company, where professionals, like me and my senior colleagues, are building the future, building many more Airtels out of the present Airtel by being entrepreneurs.

I'm not a professional alone. I'm an entrepreneur. We're extending this kind of an ethos, and building this DNA, across all our leadership team members. They actually get a bonus by being entrepreneurial, by taking risks and doing experiments that no one else tries. More often than not, they succeed. Even

> "The culture we built, and the DNA we built, was very change-oriented. If you change faster, you'll be able to get on top of the market and your competitors."

if they don't, we don't mind it, because we need to be different. We need to achieve success, not by money or funding, but by intellectual capability.

Manoj Kohli is the CEO of Bharti Airtel, a leading integrated telecom company in India. Mr Kohli joined Bharti in 2002 as head of the mobile services unit. As CEO and Joint Managing Director, he heads the integrated telco, which includes mobile services, telemedia services, enterprise services and international operations.

These insights are drawn from interviews published by Harvard Business Press in Built for Change*, an exclusive edition of the Lessons Learned series and the result of a content partnership between IBM and 50 Lessons.*

The path forward

New models for customer-focused leadership

Cristene Gonzalez-Wertz

As businesses take their first tentative steps after the recent global economic shocks, marketing, sales and service executives must confront a set of new market forces exposed by the downturn. Consumer behavior has fundamentally changed, the world is increasingly digital and the viability of existing business models is being challenged. Customer relationship management (CRM) professionals must quickly focus on developing the customer insight and digital-channel leadership that will allow them to transform customer experience, open new markets and reduce organizational complexity.

The depth of the recession and the likely residual effects raise significant questions about the viability of old ways of doing business. Are the tried and true business models – those that created the economic boom of the early part of the past decade – still valid? Do these models reflect the way consumers want to engage with businesses? Do businesses have the right data at the right time and in the format required to generate strategic insights that drive real growth?

To answer these questions and more, the IBM Institute for Business Value surveyed nearly 500 customer relationship management executives – across roles,

FIGURE 1 **BREAKDOWN OF CRM STUDY RESPONDENTS**

The 2009 IBM Customer Relationship Management Study methodology

Research overview: In May 2009, IBM, in conjunction with the Economist Intelligence Unit, conducted a web survey of 478 CRM executives in 66 countries to define the emerging state of marketing, sales and service.

Interviews by industry

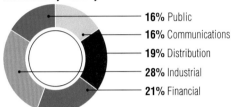

- **16%** Public
- **16%** Communications
- **19%** Distribution
- **28%** Industrial
- **21%** Financial

Interviews by title

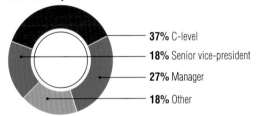

- **37%** C-level
- **18%** Senior vice-president
- **27%** Manager
- **18%** Other

Interviews by function

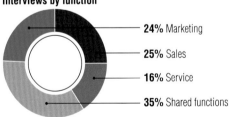

- **24%** Marketing
- **25%** Sales
- **16%** Service
- **35%** Shared functions

industries and management responsibilities – in more than 60 countries. Our goal was to assess the state of marketing, sales and service and to define the paths for leadership in the emerging digital age.

The 2009 IBM Customer Relationship Management Study reveals that 80 percent of global CRM leaders believe they are prepared to handle the demands of the new economic environment. However, even though most expect recovery to begin no later than mid-to-late 2010, they cite the economy as the force most likely to affect business decisions and results for the foreseeable future.

Our research across multiple industries and geographies shows that emerging market forces are likely to drive a major transformation of business models and customer engagement functions over the next few years. Thus customer interactions will have to be reshaped to address the changing dynamics of how people make purchasing decisions and engage with companies.

At the forefront of change is the explosion in digital information. Consider, for example, that more data was created in 2009 than in the past 5,000 years combined.[1] And with the world's four billion cell phones, two billion Internet users, 33 billion RFID tags and many billions of transistors adding data to the stream minute by minute, the information clutter will not abate anytime soon.[2]

Companies are inundated with so much information that making sound decisions is becoming exponentially more difficult. The challenge is to mine these large mountains of data to find those nuggets of information and to enable those actions that add real customer value. Closing this gap – from insight to action across any and all channels – is the foundation for new paths to leadership.

Today's marketing, sales and service leaders, regardless of industry, business model or geography must:
- Listen across a wide array of connected people and things;
- Learn by collecting, connecting and reducing data into insight and accelerating that process through the use of technology;
- Engage the customer simply and directly, moving seamlessly from decision to action in the business processes that drive relevant experiences;
- Harvest these interactions to continuously improve customer engagement through all channels, devices and people.

A greater ability to mine data, leverage analytics and create an effective communications platform opens the door for three categories of leaders to emerge by 2012:

Customer insight leaders, who optimize myriad data, transform it into something useful and create measurable value;

Digital channel leaders, who harness new methods of creating value through customer interactions and new products, services and business models in an always-on digital world;

New era leaders, who incorporate the best practices from both of the above categories.

Further, these three segments will be able to choose – based on the business conditions they face and the market positions they want to occupy – from among three distinct levers to increase their potential for differentiation: radical cost and complexity reduction; innovative market making; and strategic service delivery. Depending on its needs, a company may choose just one lever or combine elements from all three.

Cost and complexity reduction takes costs out of business to make operations leaner, more flexible and more accessible to customers. Innovative market making focuses on social business design to engage customers, partners and suppliers in creating value. It provides the opportunity – or imperative – to co-create solutions and products alongside customers, partners and vendors – and even competitors. Strategic service delivery uses all available channels to improve the customer experience. Whether the customer chooses to call the contact center, visit a retail outlet or branch, find the answer via the website or engage through social tools such as microblogging, strategic service considers the customer's goals and enables customer success. It optimizes every channel to be responsive and engaging – however, whenever, wherever and why-ever the customer chooses. It also allows the customer to move seamlessly from channel to channel – for instance, moving from the web to the contact center or to a retailer to purchase what he or she has found.

In the data-intensive, customer-friendly digital age, leaders will be defined by how they develop and leverage insight to respond to ever-changing consumer demands. They will do this while embracing new digital communications for sales, service and marketing. Whether they focus on differentiating themselves through customer insight, digital channels or both, they will realize the benefits by taking quick, decisive action. In this paper, we detail the categories of leadership and the levers that can be used to get there.

The economy and market forces

Even though most of those we surveyed feel the worst of the economic downturn has passed, they still expect overall economic conditions to be a big factor for at least the next two to three years (see Figure 2). They foresee that there will be less "easy money" available for large capital expenditures. Respondents also expect increased competition – not only from new entrants in emerging markets, but also from the heightened pursuit of fewer consumer dollars. They recognize that the "old days" of open wallets and liberal credit are gone – at least for awhile.

Beyond the economy, increased competition and access to capital, three factors indicate a need for change: new customer demands; the increased prevalence of digital information; and the rise of new economies as population and wealth distributions shift across the globe. Other external factors, such as volatile energy prices and sustainability demands, are critical to specific industries but are not global forces in the manner of the others.

The extent and speed with which most companies can move beyond the economy and focus on other factors that challenge performance depends more on where they are located than what they do. For example, when leaders were asked to assess the external factors most likely to influence business decisions by 2012, only 36 percent of US marketing, sales and service executives cited the economy, compared with 67 percent in emerging economies, 63 percent in the UK and 48 percent in Australia and Singapore. A number of factors play into these numbers, but, in general, those countries hardest hit by massive layoffs and financial institution collapse (such as the UK) are likely to be more wary long term of letting their focus stray too far from economic conditions when making decisions.

> Faced with a deluge of choices, consumers have the capability to tune messages in or out.

By contrast, the US places almost as much emphasis on access to capital and the digital information explosion (27 percent) in 2012 as on the economy, significantly above the 16 percent for respondents overall and more than three times those in China and India. In China, India and emerging markets, increased competition and access to capital are projected to be significant market factors.

While the global focus is heavily directed toward the economy and increased competition, we feel three forces that flew under the collective radar of our respondents deserve considerably more attention: new business models; new customer demands; and the digital information explosion.

FIGURE 2 **SELECTED MARKET FORCES BY 2012**

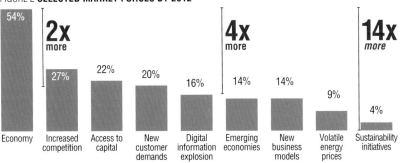

Source: *IBM Institute for Business Value 2009 CRM Leadership Study.*

Three key drivers of change

Today's empowered and enlightened consumer is driving marketplace changes that have a significant impact on companies' go-to-market and service approaches. Consumers are more informed, aware and concerned about products. Faced with a deluge of product information and choices, they have the ability to tune messages in or out. They purchase products and services through an ever-growing and changing number of channels. They consume a wider range of products than ever before, and they are not easily segmented into categories or descriptions.[3]

It was, therefore, surprising that three external forces related to satisfying the needs and wants of today's consumers were not more highly rated by survey respondents: new business models (with a 14 percent response); increased customer demands (20 percent); and the digital information explosion (16 percent).

New business models: Many traditional business models are in decline – or are failing. The financial services industry, for example, has been propped up by government intervention. Health care, regardless of geography, is outstripping the resources allocated for its delivery. Many newspapers, slow to respond to the digital era, are stopping the presses permanently. And the music industry now has a radically different primary distribution system. The message is clear: Outdated business models must be transformed to meet the evolving demands of the digital age consumer.

Increased customer demands: It isn't only a digitally savvy and informed customer who is changing the CRM outlook. Executives must also address a redistribution of wealth and population. Dramatic growth in emerging markets is being offset by stagnation, or even declines, in regions that have been among the wealthiest in the world (see Figure 3). Further, many consumers in the developed markets have radically changed their spending habits. Responding to these dynamics will be critical for companies that aspire to market leadership.

Digital information explosion: It is not simply the volume of digital information, but the effects on traditional media models and on the business

FIGURE 3 **AGGREGATE PURCHASING POWER OF A SHIFTING GLOBAL POPULATION**

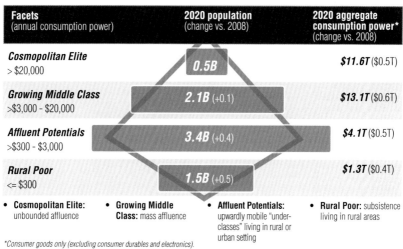

Facets (annual consumption power)	2020 population (change vs. 2008)	2020 aggregate consumption power* (change vs. 2008)
Cosmopolitan Elite > $20,000	**0.5B**	**$11.6T** ($0.5T)
Growing Middle Class >$3,000 - $20,000	**2.1B** (+0.1)	**$13.1T** ($0.6T)
Affluent Potentials >$300 - $3,000	**3.4B** (+0.4)	**$4.1T** ($0.5T)
Rural Poor <= $300	**1.5B** (+0.5)	**$1.3T** ($0.4T)

- **Cosmopolitan Elite:** unbounded affluence
- **Growing Middle Class:** mass affluence
- **Affluent Potentials:** upwardly mobile "under-classes" living in rural or urban setting
- **Rural Poor:** subsistence living in rural areas

Consumer goods only (excluding consumer durables and electronics).
Source: IBM Institute for Business Value analysis; World Bank, "Bottom Billion;" World Resources Institute; United Nations.

at large that are driving change. For example, airlines and hotels are affected by new technologies that allow virtual meetings, potentially reducing demand for their services. Compact disc and DVD sales have declined as customers express their preference for digitally delivered content. Consumers are searching online for ways to save money across their entire spending portfolio.

Businesses will need to harness these forces to create usable information – listening and learning before engaging with customers to create flexible and adaptive business models. They will need to harvest what they learn and deliver content seamlessly across channels to facilitate customer interaction. Customers, on the other hand, will expect to engage the company wherever and whenever they choose and have a hand in creating products and service approaches that meet their needs – a rising phenomenon known as customer co-creation. Customers will increasingly guide organizations to less complex approaches to meet their needs. This symbiotic approach – leveraging the customer's input – is at the heart of new social business designs that drive innovative market approaches and better strategic service.

New definitions of leadership

Those companies that respond to the market forces driving change and understand on a fundamental level how customer preferences are evolving are those most likely to assume leadership positions over the next few years. The optimum path for leadership will be determined by where and how companies apply their knowledge. Ultimately, we believe three categories of leadership will emerge to separate innovative enterprises from the pack: customer insight leaders; digital channel leaders; and

FIGURE 4 **LEADERSHIP ATTRIBUTES**

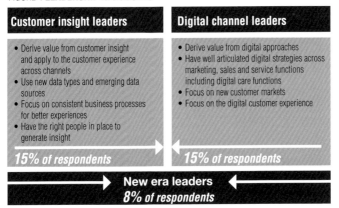

Customer insight leaders

- Derive value from customer insight and apply to the customer experience across channels
- Use new data types and emerging data sources
- Focus on consistent business processes for better experiences
- Have the right people in place to generate insight

15% of respondents

Digital channel leaders

- Derive value from digital approaches
- Have well articulated digital strategies across marketing, sales and service functions including digital care functions
- Focus on new customer markets
- Focus on the digital customer experience

15% of respondents

New era leaders
8% of respondents

Source: IBM Institute for Business Value 2009 CRM Leadership Study.

new era leaders (see Figure 4). Companies using these leadership models are likely to show clear performance differences over those that do not.

Customer insight leaders account for 15 percent of the companies we surveyed. They are most adept at capturing, using and deriving value not only by generating insight but by moving from insight to concrete business actions through their people and business processes. They are expert in the use of emerging data sources, such as GPS, web surfing and social network analysis. Instead of simply collecting the data, they use it. They leverage the right people to build and disseminate insight across the organization 83 percent of the time – versus 15 percent among non-leaders. They are better equipped to leverage the drivers of loyalty, with 67 percent reporting they understand loyalty versus 22 percent of non-leaders. They have solid business processes to support customer experience more often – 75 percent for leaders versus 15 percent for others.

These leaders start with what the customer wants and tune processes by channels – allowing better measurement and better customer experiences. They also take the opportunity to learn from customers to create better experiences by addressing what is wrong in the current experience. They are more than three times more likely to understand where targeted improvements can improve the customer experience by delivering on "moments of truth." Customer insight leaders innovate with greater success because they understand where cost can be removed without adversely affecting customers. They center the changes on improving service strategically. They mine customer dialogues for needed improvements and for new ideas to reshape the business.

Digital channel leaders encompass about 15 percent of the respondents and outperform even the customer insight leaders on elements of digital and multichannel strategies. Almost two thirds of digital leaders reported use of a multichannel strategy versus 54 percent of customer insight leaders. That gap holds for digital marketing strategies – 81 percent of digital channel leaders report having an effective digital marketing strategy compared with 65 percent of customer insight leaders. Another area of difference is the embrace of digital service strategies, where 68 percent of digital leaders advanced a service strategy that encouraged customers to be served in the lowest-cost channel to meet their needs. The research showed 56 percent of the customer insight leaders used a similar strategy. In particular, digital channel leaders were more focused on mining online conversations for insight – with 33 percent of them indicating an interest in doing so.

> Customers will expect to have a hand in developing products and service approaches that meet their needs through co-creation.

New era leaders, at 8 percent of the sample, are the rarest of the new generation of innovators, employing both customer insight and digital channels to respond at the highest levels in both arenas. They derive value from the same sources as digital channel and customer insight leaders – analytics and emerging data sources. New era leaders are four times more likely than the sample average to have the right analytic tools in place and to have an effective e-commerce strategy. They represent an extremely powerful combination of having insight and knowing exactly what to do with it, digitally as well as across all channels.

Regardless of which leadership model they employ, outperformers tend to share specific characteristics (see sidebar). They are rarely defined by role, geography, industry or business model, but are identified through their willingness to take bold action and to act outside of traditional boundaries.

FIGURE 5 **NEW ERA LEADERS VERSUS ALL OTHER STUDY PARTICIPANTS**

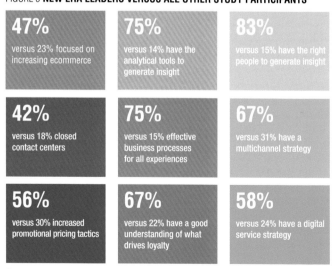

47% versus 23% focused on increasing ecommerce	**75%** versus 14% have the analytical tools to generate insight	**83%** versus 15% have the right people to generate insight
42% versus 18% closed contact centers	**75%** versus 15% effective business processes for all experiences	**67%** versus 31% have a multichannel strategy
56% versus 30% increased promotional pricing tactics	**67%** versus 22% have a good understanding of what drives loyalty	**58%** versus 24% have a digital service strategy

Source: IBM Institute for Business Value 2009 CRM Leadership Study.

CHARACTERISTICS OF CRM LEADERSHIP

The CRM study shows that leaders, regardless of category, have a bias for action. They understand how to position their companies to withstand the rigors of an economic downturn. They provide their people with the proper tools and analytics. Leaders are more apt to use insight to determine what drives customer actions. Across industries, geographies and business models, they share common traits. They include:

- Leaders across models are more likely to take difficult actions early in an economic cycle, allowing them to move forward quickly. For example, during the recession, they were 20 percent more likely to have made staff and budget reductions than others. Similarly, they focused on scaling back or slowing projects where possible.
- Outperformers recognize the value in focusing across the channels to make changes based on both efficiency and customer satisfaction. For example, leaders were twice as likely as others to have shifted into e-commerce and reduced contact centers.
- Leaders are two and a half times more likely than others to use insight to drive growth and three and a half times more likely to have the right people and competencies in place. Overall, they are more likely to understand the customer lifecycle and to use insight for repeatable business processes for better customer experiences by a four to one margin over their peers.
- Leaders understand customer loyalty better by a factor of three times – and do not equate it with a loyalty program. They understand, for example, that a discount program does not maintain loyalty; it maintains frequency. They know, however, that loyalty comes from making customers more engaged, smarter, better connected and better informed.
- Leaders are four times more likely to understand where they have the opportunity to learn and create better experiences by fixing what customers tell them is wrong. They know that when an organization can learn specifically where it needs to improve, it can create better experiences and richer, deeper customer connections.

Leaders in each category exhibited these traits, but new era leaders were substantially above average in every aspect (see Figure 5).

In all categories, leaders provide the necessary tools to create impact. The gaps between leaders and others are significant when these tools are present. Only 20 percent of sales executives report they have the critical tools to do their jobs effectively. Yet our findings show that well-equipped sales leaders deliver two and a half times the customer value of their peers. Marketing is the least well equipped, especially in analytics – less than 20 percent of respondents regularly receive analytics, compared with 63 percent for leaders (see Figure 6).

Lack of proper tools is akin to trying to drive a car at high speed and with great precision with only one hand and no instrumentation. Similarly, leaders

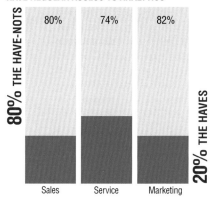

FIGURE 6 **20 PERCENT OF CRM PROFESSIONALS HAVE REGULAR ACCESS TO ANALYTICS**

80% THE HAVE-NOTS

80%   74%   82%

Sales   Service   Marketing

20% THE HAVES

Source: IBM Institute for Business Value 2009 CRM Leadership Study.

focus on having the right personnel in critical roles to generate and distribute insight. These people are crucial not only to creating insight but to making it consumable and actionable for the organization.

Three levers for success

In the data-intensive digital age, companies with leadership aspirations must decide on the levers that will provide the most opportunity for differentiation. We asked participants what approaches they would take to differentiate themselves in the next three years. Entering new customer markets was the most prevalent option, selected by nearly half of respondents. Improving service was next, at 45 percent. New channel strategies and customer co-creation were the next big areas of differentiation, closely followed by becoming a low-cost provider and regaining trust, each identified by about one third of respondents. However, with areas of differentiation reflecting a wide group of responses, it can helpful to group them into levers that reflect the intent and organization's overriding need. This leads to three core levers: cost and complexity reduction; strategic service delivery; and innovative market making (see Figure 7). Of these, cost and complexity reduction is often the least customer-centric path, while strategic service delivery and innovative market making offer progressively more customer engagement.

FIGURE 7 **THREE CORE LEVERS TO CREATE THE PATH FORWARD**

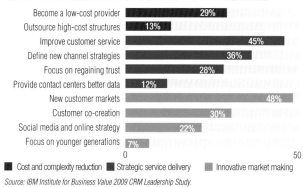

Become a low-cost provider — 29%
Outsource high-cost structures — 13%
Improve customer service — 45%
Define new channel strategies — 36%
Focus on regaining trust — 28%
Provide contact centers better data — 12%
New customer markets — 48%
Customer co-creation — 30%
Social media and online strategy — 22%
Focus on younger generations — 7%

0   50

■ Cost and complexity reduction   ■ Strategic service delivery   ■ Innovative market making

Source: IBM Institute for Business Value 2009 CRM Leadership Study.

Cost and complexity reduction makes operations more flexible, leaner and more accessible to customers. While traditionally treated as an internal measure, increasingly the benefits of cost and complexity reduction, especially through use of digital channels, can reduce the costs of serving customers. This is a sizable opportunity – as 66 percent of the respondents did not think their company was fully able to offer a digital service strategy that allowed them to focus on cost-to-serve.

Businesses tend to get more complex over time. Optimization across channels and business functions can be challenging when speed is needed to enter new markets or improve service. This speed can actually undermine effective design in preference for "getting it done." However, creating and sustaining leadership in today's economic environment will require businesses to make complex processes more responsive to customers and global business conditions. By making complexity reduction a goal from the outset, organizations can set up the right processes and channel optimization when entering into new customer markets and when delivering improved service. The organization becomes simpler, faster, smarter and more flexible. It becomes as effective as it is efficient. Lastly, cost and complexity reduction can be critical in freeing up capital to support and sustain these emerging operations.

Innovative market making changes the way organizations enter and develop new markets. It focuses on co-creation of value and on social media to engage customers and understand interactions with vendors, government bodies and competitors. This social framework allows companies to detect and predict changes in market conditions and customer demands and to respond accordingly. Conceptually, market making uses this collaborative paradigm to deliver new products and services to new markets faster and with greater flexibility.

Innovative market making has the external social media components we have come to expect, but it has also enabled internal collaboration – making it easier to find information, people and ideas across the company. However, it also recognizes that regardless of how many employees a company has, great ideas, technologies and paths to interaction are often found outside the enterprise. For example, years ago IBM physicists realized that a laser could make a clean precise cut, allowing them to engrave our name in human hair. How could this have commercial value? Well, someone else figured out that this approach could, in fact, be used to create a smooth cut in the sclera of the human eye, leading to laser vision correction. Other companies brought the technology to market and, by 2009, it represented a $US2.5 billion market in the US.[4]

Strategic service delivery encompasses activities that improve customer interactions through new channels to engage in dialogue creation. Strategic service delivery provides the interactive and data-driven means to learn from and share with customers how companies meet their needs. It also allows a company to improve customer convenience. One example of this is using the Internet to deliver improved service and troubleshooting techniques. We no longer need the CD that came with a printer to install drivers, as we can download them. Similarly, when individuals can categorize their credit card spending through tagging and graphing, they gain a much richer picture of their financial activity and can undertake changes if they so desire.

Strategic service delivery also allows customers to lead other customers to better decisions. Through ratings and reviews, whether on a company-owned site or on a social network like Facebook, customers express their preferences and brand connections, allowing those around them to leverage the wisdom of the crowds who have faced the same purchase decision. Each path forward meets certain conditions in the market better than others. These must be matched with organizational strategy to determine the correct path (see Figure 8).

FIGURE 8 **HOW LEADERS CAN APPLY THE THREE LEVERS FOR SUCCESS**

	Customer insight leaders	Digital channel leaders	New era leaders
Cost and complexity reduction	• Focus on business process to apply insight more rapidly to all channels • Understand where to remove cost without impacting experiences	• Reduce marketing contact costs • Simplify sales process • Reduce cost in the service processes through self-service and guided approaches	• Use insight to drive cost reduction across the CRM functions and understand the dependencies • Can measure the success of channel switching programs
Strategic service delivery	• Understand and can measure consistent channel delivery • Focus on the full customer life-cycle	• Deliver web-based content that engages across customer life-cycle • Understand cost to serve in digital channels	• Provide multipoint measurable access for service delivery across the customer life-cycle • Can combine channel specific metrics into customer-focused metrics
Innovative market making	• Actively listen and learn from the voice of the customer across channels • Collaborate with customers on products, services	• Use multiple forms of social media to engage • Harness the power of the web-based customer advocates to engage potential customers	• Deliver new digital offerings that enable better customer value at favorable costs • Use new forms of testing and measurement to collect web-based feedback in real-time

Source: IBM Institute for Business Value 2009 CRM Leadership Study.

Regardless of the path selected, however, new leadership models will be needed, to enable each path and to reflect the increasingly information-rich digital world. These models determine where the organization will invest in improvement, as well as the lens through which it will direct its human and operational assets such as process and technology.

CONCLUSION: THE PATH FORWARD

In examining the paths chosen by digital channel, customer insight and new era leaders, we find that both market making and strategic service require four specific areas of action, with each sharing a key optimization point (see Figure 9). Companies desiring to attain leadership along these paths must:

Listen: Sense and extract data from people and things, while reducing it to actionable information;

Learn: Target content delivery in a way that is customer-preferred and relevant across all channels and opportunities. This enables the channeling of insight into the organization to create well-crafted customer experiences;

Engage: Enable the organization to engage the customer and the community continuously in sharing and creating value. This entails enabling all media to support the customers and the organization;

Harvest: Deliver information that improves the way customer management functions plan and execute their work, including enabling better performance across functions to deliver value.

FIGURE 9: **AREAS OF LEADERSHIP ACTION**

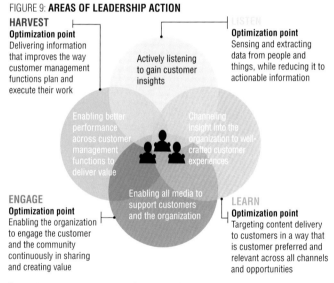

Source: IBM Institute for Business Value 2009 CRM Leadership Study.

Listening and learning are central to customer insight development and application. Engaging and harvesting are core tenets of strategic service – and especially digital delivery.

Customer insight drives success with any of the three levers. While the listen-learn-engage-harvest paradigm defines the continuum of activities, the approach relies on defining what insight is needed and when and how it can be applied. To create strategic leadership in this arena, however, requires diligent assessment and planning (see Table 1).

TABLE 1 **DEVELOPING LISTEN, LEARN, ENGAGE AND HARVEST COMPETENCIES**

ACTIVITY	ACTIONS	ACCELERATORS
LISTEN	• Document and redefine the customer experience. • Identify moments of truth based on customer input, front-line personnel feedback and publicly available data. Identify emerging data sources that deliver valuable information. • Look at as broad a range of information sources as the team can handle.	• Consider working with a business partner who has a predefined event and moment-of-truth library. • Look for vendors who offer deep mathematical expertise and models to validate findings and offer templated approaches. • Listening to the voice of the customer is not only a forward-facing activity. One of the advantages of web-based traceability is that companies can go back over a period of time and develop an increased understanding of their customers as a starting point. Similarly, using semantic engines to mine companies' rich contact center data can drive increased insight without primary research.
LEARN	• Apply the findings of listening activities in combination with sales performance and industry benchmarking to create new business models, products, services and interactions. • Focus on improving moments of truth as a priority. Set learning objectives for every interaction – including outcomes, metrics and customer success criteria. • Evaluate the technologies and infrastructures that provide the best support in delivering improved customer interactions. • Include these in a business case for any necessary investments.	• Use pre-built business case templates that can be customized to the organization's need rather than starting from scratch. Working from well-defined assumptions and architectures can strip weeks out of delivery timing. • Testing models should be defined enough to allow rigor, but not so complex as to prevent pursuing new ideas.
ENGAGE	• Enable customers to participate in dialogues, not just receive content. Pursue multiple ways for customers to rate, review, share and create content. • Focus on cross-channel continuity for experiences, processes and content delivery. • Develop measurement approaches as well as predictive analytics that focus on customer experience and customer objectives as well as cost and revenue.	• Select methods and tools that are flexible with minimal reliance on other parts of the organization for enablement. • Focus on sharing knowledge across the organization.
HARVEST	• Continually review listen, learn and engagement results across the organization to update the experiences, business processes, moments of truth, channel interactions and service specifications. • Share wherever possible with the customer.	• Dashboards with customized views allow multiple parties across CRM to see only the data they need based on their role and permissions. • Use informal and formal means to share results and ideas. Human interaction still counts. • The digital era has brought visibility as well to experts around the globe. Seek out those improvement approaches and share ideas. These experts may not be in the organization, but are often wiling to engage with you.

Source: IBM Institute for Business Value 2009 CRM Leadership Study.

ARE YOU READY?

Getting started depends upon an honest assessment of where you are, how you want to lead and how you want to get there. You must make a realistic assessment of your business model and its customer-focused strategy implications and determine the level of transformation needed. To assess your readiness:

- Determine which levers best match your organization based on your specific needs.
- Examine the existing business model and revenue generation approaches and compare them with the experiences that customers want.
- Define and address any gaps in the four areas that enable you to focus on the customer experience – listening, learning, engaging and harvesting.
- Identify the current and new metrics that would allow specific improvements to the ability to define and improve experiences across the channels.
- Assess the abilities of your core organization for development of customer insight and digital channel delivery. Determine the effectiveness of existing multichannel and digital strategies to deliver your needs. Are they tightly integrated across functions? Are they delivering results?
- Realign metrics across the organization around the desired customer experiences, the revenue that can be generated by delivering them, the insight needed to develop and maintain them and the channels that will deliver them. Create cross-functional road maps that enable the desired business model, products, services and markets to be effectively developed, deployed and measured.
- Create specific organizational change plans for the people who will deliver the strategy and develop the organization's leadership potential.

ABOUT THE AUTHOR

Cristene Gonzalez-Wertz is the Global CRM Research Leader for the IBM Institute for Business Value. She has a background in marketing strategy, science and transformation and has more than 20 years' real-world business and consulting experience. Her experience spans retail, media and communications, financial services, telematics and travel in development of customer-centric solutions. She is considered a social media maven by clients and colleagues and can be found on her blog, Twitter, Facebook and other social media spaces. She can be reached at cristene@us.ibm.com.

CONTRIBUTORS

Dan Hirschbueler, Global CRM Service Line Leader, IBM Global Business Services; Eric Lesser, Research Director, IBM Institute for Business Value, IBM Global Business Services; Scott Jenkins, Associate Partner, IBM Applications Innovation; Adam Cutler, User Experience Director, IBM Interactive; and Aparna Betigeri, CRM Managing Consultant, IBM Global Business Services.

REFERENCES

1   Weigend, Andreas. "The Social Data Revolution(s)." Now, New, Next: The Monitor Talent Group Blog. Harvard Business Publishing. May 20, 2009. http://blogs. harvardbusiness.org/now-new-next/2009/05/the-social-data-revolution.html

2   "6 Billion Cell Phone Users by 2013?" DarkVision Hardware. February 16, 2009. http://www.dvhardware.net/article33384.html; Internet Usage Statistics. The Internet Big Picture. Internetworldstats.com. http://www.internetworldstats.com/stats.htm

3   Blissett, Guy. "Establishing trust through traceability: Protect and empower your brand for today's 'Omni Consumer.'" IBM Institute for Business Value. 2007. http://www-935.ibm.com/services/us/gbs/bus/pdf/g510-6621-01-traceability.pdf

4   "IBM's Excimer Laser Eye Surgery Inventors to be Inducted into National Inventors Hall of Fame: Laser Eye Surgery Improves Vision for More Than 5 Million People Within 8 Years of Commercialization." IBM. May 16, 2002. http://domino.watson.ibm.com/comm/pr.nsf/pages/news.20020515_invent.html; "In Mature LASIK Market, Competition, Recession Bring Down Prices." *Laser Eye News.* September 7, 2009. http://lasereyenews.blogspot.com

Insights Customer-focused innovation

More than 1,000 CEOs engaged with IBM in the discussions that underpin *The Enterprise of the Future*. In a series of follow-up video interviews conducted for the study by 50 Lessons, the world's premier multimedia business resource – and in interviews previously conducted by 50 Lessons – some of the world's top business leaders speak to the study's key themes.

Ivan Seidenberg, CEO of Verizon, on innovating by anticipating customer needs.

If you look at the last eight, nine or ten years, our industry, our company sits right in the middle of the juxtaposition between the customer and those who build and deploy technology. What we have really had to figure out is how to get closer to the customer. And the closer we get to the customer, the easier it is for us to participate in the whole idea of innovation, which leads to growth of the business.

Let's take a couple of examples of what we do well and what we have learned over the years. If we look at our business, we've been in business for a hundred years. We're primarily a business where you pick up the phone and you make a phone call; you make a plain-old voice call. We have now moved into an era where data and wireless voice are the dominant services we give to our customers.

The whole idea of being able to deliver customer-friendly, value-creating products and services to customers is something that we've really had to work very hard on. If you go back 15 to 20 years, when we introduced data, we had a hard time figuring out how to get the modems, DSL and ISDN right. And as I talk, you can see what we have are all technical engineering terms to describe a shift from the voice business to the data business.

We could have innovated faster and better had we been more focused on giving customers what they wanted. We did this much better with wireless. Wireless is also a voice business, giving people the ability to make phone calls, but the idea of very robust handsets, great coverage and good quality service enabled us to create exciting products and services for customers and made a big difference in the way they saw the company.

Innovation is all about growth. It's all about differentiation. And it really is all about anticipating what the customer's looking for, as opposed to what's easy to do when you produce these kinds of new ideas from inside a business. You need to make sure that innovation is driven from the outside in.

> "The closer we get to the customer, the easier it is for us to participate in the whole idea of innovation, which leads to growth of the business."

How you anticipate needs to drive good services is always a difficult issue, but you have to be a student. You have to be a student of your customers and of the technology, and you have to always put yourself in a position of learning. You need multiple sources within your own company to bring ideas to the middle.

As an executive, what you're always worrying about is making sure you get that right balance. What I notice in our business today is that we get a tremendous amount of input from people who build technology – box manufacturers, consumer electronics, suppliers – and they're always bringing to us what they think are the next great things. But generally it's the next great technical thing. What you find is that if you have your people sitting very close to the customers, you can quickly determine whether a given idea has some merit with the marketplace.

The issue for us is to have checks and balances, to have a strong marketing and sales organization that speaks to the needs of the customers in ways that aren't just a reflection of what is possible as it is explained to us by manufacturers and suppliers.

Ivan Seidenberg is Chairman and Chief Executive Officer of the premier network company Verizon Communications Inc. Verizon is the second-largest US telecommunications services provider.

K. Vaman Kamath, non-executive Chairman and former CEO and Managing Director of ICICI Bank Limited, on the value of focusing on customer convenience.

Around the year 2000, if I were to look at our typical bank branch and the number of customers who came in and transacted, I would estimate we had less than half a million customers and maybe a little more than 100 branches. So we weren't very large. Ninety-five percent of the transactions happened in the branch. The remaining 5 percent of transactions happened over a few stray ATMs we had.

The ATM is a machine that can be plonked anywhere, as long as you can ensure connectivity. In the whole of India there were maybe 100-odd machines. We said, "In year one, we will roll out 1,000 machines, at an average of three machines a day." Now, that doesn't sound large by Western standards. But to put it in context, to roll out an ATM in India you had to allow for three levels of redundancy in connectivity, because connectivity was so bad. And, of course, you had to make sure there was power all the time; otherwise your customers would get irate. It was because of this situation that my customers would say, "Nobody has ever used an ATM, and nobody will." We responded, "Nobody uses an ATM because there are no ATMs. Let's see what happens when you have ATMs."

Then we bet on the Internet, because we were large players in the distributive space. We wanted to push the Internet as a mainline channel. Again, we met the same level of scepticism: "Who's going to use the Internet in this country? People don't have access to a computer."

Then there was the call center. The argument was that customers like to go to the branch, to sit there, talk and then get their business done. My argument was: That's not going to happen here, because it's a busy branch. We want the customer to transact, be satisfied and then leave, because he won't have time to sit and talk. Neither will the bank officer. That's going to be the new paradigm. You need a call center, where he can talk and can get his answer.

"If you believe something is of convenience to your customer, and you can deliver that convenience at a fraction of the cost, the customer will seek you out."

To me, the ATM, the Internet and the call center are all convenience points. The Internet today accounts for something like 25 percent of transactions, which you would have thought impossible in a country like India. Then you have the rest split between the ATMs – about 40 percent or so – and the balance is through the call center.

The lesson here is that if you believe something is of convenience to your customer, and you can deliver that convenience at a fraction of the cost, the customer will seek you out. The customer will work with you in that context. In our case, we have been able to keep costs low and provide better service to the customer through multiple channels. It becomes a huge selling point in the way we talk to our customers, particularly the young Indian. India is a country with 70 percent of the population under the age of 35. The young Indian, who is now savvy in all these tools, whether it is the use of the computer, cell phone or ATM, becomes a natural to do business with us.

K. Vaman Kamath is non-executive Chairman and former Managing Director and CEO of ICICI Bank, India's second-largest bank. Headquartered in Mumbai, ICICI is India's largest private bank, with more than 1,250 branches located in more than 20 countries.

Yuehong Fu, General Manager of Golden Resource New Yansha Mall, on intelligent customer service.
During the past 20 years, the commercial services industry has entered a period of rapid development in China. New Yansha Group is committed to raising the level of technology used throughout this entire industry. For example, the integrated information management system we developed for the Golden Resource Shopping Mall project provides an online network for hundreds of shops and banks. Using this system, consumers can swipe a range of credit, debit and ATM cards while shopping, and we can collect market data for research and services purposes. When implemented, the level of complexity of this system was unique in China. In fact, the implementation of such a large-scale IT system has elevated the use of technology by commercial enterprises in Beijing and throughout the entire nation.

Since the beginning, we have attached great importance to the use of technology. The bigger the shopping mall, the more complexity is involved and consequently the more difficult it is for people to achieve results without the aid of technology.

We had a strong partnership with IBM and decided to introduce an IT system while preparing for the development of the shopping mall. We also received support from a range of Chinese banks. Now we have several hundred point-of-service terminals connected to our information system. This is an example of how the system has improved our efficiency by making all contracts and sales information accessible via the network.

> "Using this technology-based system, we can conduct data analyses that show us sales data hour by hour ... we know when a consumer has come to the mall ... and we can predict the stores that will survive and those that will not."

Using this technology-based system, we are able to understand sales trends. For example, we can conduct data analyses that show us sales data hour by hour and day by day. With this data we know when a consumer has come to the mall, and we can predict the stores that will survive and those that will not. With the analysis complete, we can make practical adjustments and implement real business changes.

Today all of our people depend on our information system to carry out their day-to-day work. The development of this information system has also guided the development of the entire shopping mall sector in China. Before our opening most information systems were used only for supermarkets and department stores. The system we developed set a new standard for shopping centers and especially for large-scale shopping centers. Versions of our system are now being implemented in many cities throughout China.

It is vital that we emphasize the use of technology in our business development, and we will continue our efforts in this area. For example, we built our website and we plan to develop a peer-to-peer system for shops. At the same time, we will also have more direct contact with consumers by employing new technologies. Technology will become more and more widely used and will provide us with new ways to build bridges between shops and consumers.

Yuehong Fu is the General Manager of Golden Resource New Yansha Mall, the flagship project of the New Yansha Group, a pioneering state-owned company set up by the Beijing Municipal Government and responsible for the operation of state-owned assets, primarily in the real estate and retail sectors.

These insights are drawn from interviews published by Harvard Business Press in Built for Change, *an exclusive edition of the Lessons Learned series and the result of a content partnership between IBM and 50 Lessons.*

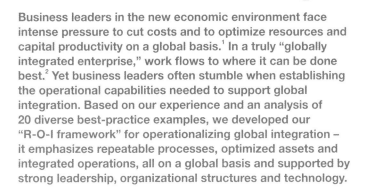

Strategies for enabling global integration

Dave Lubowe, Judith Cipollari,
Patrick Antoine and Amy Blitz

Business leaders in the new economic environment face
intense pressure to cut costs and to optimize resources and
capital productivity on a global basis.[1] In a truly "globally
integrated enterprise," work flows to where it can be done
best.[2] Yet business leaders often stumble when establishing
the operational capabilities needed to support global
integration. Based on our experience and an analysis of
20 diverse best-practice examples, we developed our
"R-O-I framework" for operationalizing global integration –
it emphasizes repeatable processes, optimized assets and
integrated operations, all on a global basis and supported by
strong leadership, organizational structures and technology.

Global integration and cross-border trade are nothing new, having been driving forces in economies since before the Roman Empire. Yet globalization has
intensified dramatically in the past decade. One key reason is the revolution
in communications technology, which continues to slash the costs of trading,
transacting and interacting across even vast distances. Between 1995 and
2007, in fact, the number of transnational companies more than doubled,
from 38,000 to 79,000, and foreign subsidiaries nearly tripled, from 265,000
to 790,000.[3] During the same period, the number of cross-border M&A deals

more than doubled, from 390 to 889,[4] though this – like much else – declined in 2008.[5]

For business leaders, such changes offer a growing set of opportunities to optimize resources and capital productivity on a global basis.[6] Yet there is considerable uncertainty about how best to do this. Our research finds that while many companies are pursuing piecemeal approaches to address various processes or areas of operation, the top performers have a comprehensive, strategic view that spans the entire organization, in what we are calling an "R-O-I" framework. As preconditions for success, companies must focus on the elements of the framework concurrently. They are:

- **Repeatable processes** – eliminating inefficiency, optimizing effectiveness and managing exceptions;
- **Optimized assets** – managing core versus non-core activities, optimizing locations and establishing virtual operations;
- **Integrated operations** – optimizing global competencies via partnering and managing end-to-end processes on a global basis;
- **Foundational elements** – establishing critical support components that span leadership, organizational structure and technology.

CLOSING THE CHANGE GAP

In *The Enterprise of the Future*, we learned that in order to capitalize on global integration, CEOs are planning radical changes in their capability, knowledge and asset mix, all while focusing on diverse global strategies (see Figure 1). Indeed, 75 percent of the CEOs told us they are pursuing global strategies in order to enter new markets for customers, as well as for talent. Moreover, while a majority of CEOs are embarking on major changes to their business designs, financial outperformers are focusing more on global business designs than underperformers, underscoring the power of a global integration strategy.[7]

There is often, however, a wide gap between the vision and the reality of global integration. While eight out of ten CEOs anticipate substantial or very substantial change over the next three years, only six out of ten reported they had successfully managed change in the past, creating a "change gap" of 22 percentage points.[8]

Global integration, a key element of navigating change, is in fact quite complex, risky and challenging, both within and outside the organization. The complexity extends beyond the organization to suppliers, regulators and others dealing with national standards that are often quite different, in areas such as product safety, environmental impact and intellectual property rights – not to mention cultural issues.

Because of the risks and challenges posed here, operationalizing a global integration strategy efficiently and effectively is often what separates the winners from the also-rans. Yet, despite the growing urgency about achieving global integration, many questions remain about how best to achieve it. Even as the literature on globalization has grown tenfold, from about 500 studies throughout the 1990s to nearly 5,000 studies on the topic between 2000 and 2004, there is still a need for hard analysis regarding the best operational strategies for enabling global integration.[9]

FIGURE 1 **CEOS PLAN RADICAL CHANGES IN OPERATING MODELS TO ENABLE GLOBAL INTEGRATION, BUT STRUGGLE WITH OPERATIONALIZING THESE CHANGES**

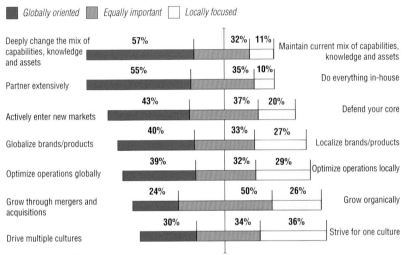

Source: IBM Global CEO Study 2008; private sector responses.

We began our investigation with these key questions: How can a global integration strategy be operationalized? What operations strategies are most effective in enabling global integration? We first examined data from *The Enterprise of the Future*, which indicated that CEOs were focused on global integration, but often struggled with how to operationalize it. We then selected 20 best-practice cases to identify patterns among the strategies used by strong global integrators. These examples were selected from *Business-Week*'s "Top Innovators List" and company reports of top performers in 2008, as well as by IBM Operations Strategy leaders.[10]

Our cases spanned Asia, Europe and the US, and diverse industries including financial services, health care, telecommunications, energy and utilities, retail, IT, automotive, oil, food and fast-moving consumer goods (see Figure 2). The 20 companies are: Alstom, Bayer Schering, British Petroleum, Cisco, Credit Suisse, Eli Lilly & Company, Goldman Sachs, IBM, Intel, Li & Fung, Mahindra and Mahindra, McDonald's, Nokia, Procter & Gamble, Samsung, Shell, Stryker, Schuler, Toyota and a major Chinese telecommunications equipment manufacturer.

As part of our analysis, we sought to determine:
- What is driving the need for global integration, and what is the business strategy?
- How is the integration being achieved – knowledge, skills, capabilities, leadership, technology?
- What are the published performance results of the company and how do these relate to global integration?

FIGURE 2 **DISTRIBUTION OF CASES BY REGION AND INDUSTRY**

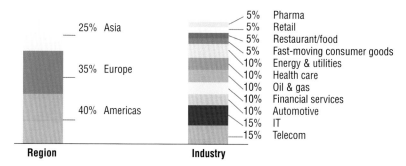

25% Asia	5% Pharma
	5% Retail
35% Europe	5% Restaurant/food
	5% Fast-moving consumer goods
	10% Energy & utilities
	10% Health care
	10% Oil & gas
	10% Financial services
40% Americas	10% Automotive
	15% IT
	15% Telecom

Region   **Industry**

Source: IBM 2009 Globally Integrated Operations study.

THE R-O-I FRAMEWORK

Our analysis of 20 best-practice cases revealed a set of clear, replicable strategies for operationalizing global integration (see Figure 3). These strategies span diverse industries and geographies, demonstrating the power of strategy over location or industry trends. In brief, each of the companies studied here focused on a global basis on three key areas of operations strategy – repeatable processes, optimized assets and integrated operations – in what we call our R-O-I framework.

FIGURE 3 **BEST PRACTICE CASES REVEAL AN "R-O-I" FRAMEWORK, DRIVEN BY LEADERSHIP, SUPPORTED BY THE ORGANIZATION AND TECHNOLOGY**

Source: IBM 2009 Globally Integrated Operations study.

Moreover, we found that successful global integration is driven by strong leadership and supported by organizational structures, as well as technology. Finally, we found that an ad hoc approach is not sufficient. In order to achieve truly globally integrated operations, it is essential to address all elements of the R-O-I framework simultaneously and well. And getting this right is an increasingly important competitive differentiator.

When we explored further the extent to which our best-practice companies focused on each of these areas, we found that 95 percent focused extensively on repeatable processes (though less so among Asian companies), while only 80 percent focused extensively on optimized assets (particularly companies from the Americas). Just 70 percent focused extensively on integrated operations (see Figure 4). Yet *The Enterprise of the Future* shows outperformers are involved extensively in global integration and are simultaneously pursuing multiple paths toward this goal – essentially spanning key elements of our R-O-I framework.

Our analysis shows that – even among best-practice cases – some areas of operations strategy needed to support global integration are better

Our analysis shows that companies that are most successful at globally integrating their operations use a comprehensive approach instead of dealing with various challenges in an ad hoc manner.

understood than others. Specifically, while establishing repeatable processes has been a long-standing objective of operations strategy, optimizing assets on a global basis and integrating operations globally are still newer, evolving and less well-understood areas of operations strategy. Moreover, while many companies are pursuing global integration in some areas, the top performers understand the need to have a systemic comprehensive approach, integrating processes, assets and operations on a global basis. This paper aims to fill this gap by exploring best practices in all of the areas identified for successful globally integrated operations.

FIGURE 4 **CASE STUDY DISTRIBUTION BY R-O-I AND BY REGION**

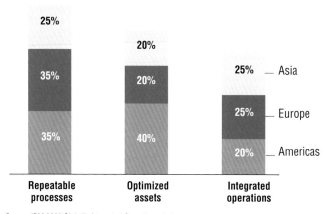

Source: IBM 2009 Globally Integrated Operations study.

R = REPEATABLE, STANDARDIZED PROCESSES

Establishing repeatable, standardized processes is a long-standing and well-understood area of operational effectiveness, from early time-and-motion studies for increasing labor productivity to subsequent Lean approaches for reducing inefficiency to Six Sigma approaches for reducing errors and quality-related problems. These led to the combined Lean Six Sigma approaches for balancing efficiency and effectiveness for optimal customer satisfaction and profitability. Ninety-five percent of our best-practice cases have extensive efforts under way to continually address the need for repeatable standardized processes on a global basis.

Eliminate inefficiencies. The first step in any strong operations strategy is to eliminate inefficiencies. The goal is to reduce cycle time through process optimization, removing all duplicate or unnecessary steps, doing things simultaneously rather than sequentially and replacing manual intervention with automation as much as possible. Moreover, the right technology must be in place, with systems interfacing end to end throughout any given process to reduce inefficiencies. To manage all of this on a global scale, common steps in the process should be pulled into a shared services model. Leaders must also be designated as responsible for specific global processes, with regional leaders in place to manage processes locally.

LI & FUNG: ELIMINATING INEFFICIENCIES

In one particularly innovative example, Li & Fung has reduced cycle times, removed inefficiencies and optimized supply chain management globally by relying on a flexible network of some 10,000 specialized manufacturers and suppliers across 40 countries, thus targeting specific customer needs without having to vertically integrate. The company uses a "pull" approach to production, producing only when orders are placed. Cotton can be purchased from America, knitted and dyed in Pakistan and sewn into garments in Cambodia – whatever configuration yields the best end result. Interestingly, the company orchestrates the supply chain for each of its customers without owning any piece of it. To manage its global network of suppliers, Li & Fung relies on sophisticated systems in its "pull" structure centering on rapid response to demand. An added bonus of this approach is the ability to track and respond to changes in customer preferences on a real-time basis.[11]

Optimize effectiveness, in terms of quality and customer satisfaction. The key here is to help ensure high-quality outputs, particularly in areas that really matter to customers. Quality controls require measurement, governance and risk mitigation, all made more complex when operating on a global scale. In measurement processes, quality checks and controls are needed at each hand-off in the process. To govern this, measurement can be either automated or manual, but it requires an owner – either an individual or a governing body – with oversight of the end-to-end process and ultimate accountability for the final product or service. Risk mitigation is also critical, with structures in place to continually assess a wide range of potential threats throughout global operations, such as systems or machines failing, as well as political, environmental, economic, societal and other risks. Every possible risk must be anticipated with back-up plans in place to handle them.

> By establishing repeatable processes, organizations can eliminate inefficiencies, optimize effectiveness and better manage exceptions when they occur.

TOYOTA: OPTIMIZING EFFECTIVENESS

A classic case is Toyota, which originated the Toyota Production System, now known more broadly as Lean Manufacturing. Using this approach, Toyota continually reduces inefficiency while verifying reliable quality via extensive automation and rigid scripts for every activity, connection and production flow in its factories. At the same time, Toyota's operations are extremely flexible and responsive to customers, minimizing inventory through just-in-time "pull" adjustments vis-à-vis demand at all stages of a production process.[12] Surprisingly, the company's strong culture of continual improvement enables this seemingly rigid system to be very adaptive and flexible, and to fix problems as they arise.

Manage exceptions. The goal is to control efficiency and quality by establishing processes that are repeatable and standardized across global operations. In this way, global demand, resources and operating expenses are all optimized globally. The challenge, however, is to achieve this while still taking into account critical cultural and geographic dimensions and managing such exceptions effectively.[13] The key is to standardize processes as much as possible, while managing local exceptions, ideally limiting these to fewer than 20 percent of all transactions.

MCDONALD'S: MANAGING EXCEPTIONS

McDonald's long ago broke down every minute step in the end-to-end process of making its French fries in order to provide consistency in the quality of food and the overall experience from Moscow to Manhattan, from Tokyo to Toledo. Still, its menus vary, with different offerings to accommodate the diverse preferences of customers around the globe, including the Maharaja Mac in India, for example, or a green tea milkshake in Japan.

O = OPTIMIZED ASSETS

Optimizing assets on a global basis is an increasingly important operations strategy, used to a high degree by 80 percent of the companies studied here. And this area of operations has undergone a rapid transformation in recent years, as the revolution in information and communications technology enables entirely new approaches to global operations, with real-time tracking, virtual supply chain management, global process integration and other operational innovations now available to connect far-flung operations. But what is the best operations strategy for navigating this new world?

Identify and manage core versus non-core processes. Being able to accurately identify where value is generated at all levels of the organization is an essential first step in optimizing assets. Strong financial systems, together with good management information, are key. Using these, business leaders can determine which activities contribute strategic value and can then eliminate weak businesses and divest where needed, moving non-core activities to shared services or outsourced solutions. This also enables a shift from fixed to variable costs, with operating models that are more flexible on a global scale and capable of moving quickly to different locations in response to changes on either the supply or demand side of operations.

> Three components of optimizing assets are: appropriately managing core versus non-core activities; optimizing locations; and establishing virtual operations.

A significant number of multinational companies are considering increased outsourcing of their IT development centers to India and China. In a similar shift away from non-core activities, pharmaceutical companies are more frequently extending their R&D processes beyond company walls to India and China in order to accelerate the pace of discovery while reducing upfront investments.[14] Similar trends are occurring in other sectors that rely heavily on R&D, including software development and consumer products.

Optimize locations. For processes that remain within the walls of the firm, companies en route to global integration must optimize locations on a global basis, putting in place the right supporting organizational structures and technology. Leading companies are now broadening their search for new locations to take advantage of new markets, talent pools and operational efficiency worldwide. Their overall goal is to locate processes where assets, talents, resources, distance to markets and other key factors of production are optimized. And as pressures to cut costs intensify, setting up operations in the most cost-effective places is essential.

Even in the absence of growing global economic activity during 2007 and 2008, companies kept expanding their geographic scope, indicating that this is a structural, not a cyclical, aspect of the economy today.[15] And this expansion has brought unprecedented levels of investment to countries previously on the periphery of the world economy.[16] The challenge, however, is to better understand the vast array of business environments, regulations, cost structures and risks (political, economic, environmental and more). These concerns can best be overcome through systematic comparisons of diverse locations based on a clear set of criteria, such as financial evaluations, investment trends and competitor analyses.

Identify and manage operations that can be performed virtually. There is a growing trend toward virtual work, with more and more employees from companies of diverse industries and sizes working from home. This can dramatically reduce corporate real estate and other associated costs, while enabling the right workers to team on projects regardless of location. It also greatly reduces the costs of travel, as well as absentee costs when, for example, an employee might otherwise need to stay home with a sick child. Offering a virtual work environment is also a growing factor in attracting and recruiting talent, ranked just below salary in one study of 1,400 CFOs.[17]

Key to these virtual organizations is a strong corporate culture that enables collaboration and sets consistent process and quality standards among team members who may never meet in person. Also critical to success is an ever-growing array of systems that enable virtual collaboration. These include: conference calls; email and instant messaging systems; online team rooms and wikis for co-developing documents; Second Life for large group sessions that mimic face-to-face meetings by assembling avatars in a virtual world; online "jams" for threaded discussions on various topics among an even larger group of participants; and a host of other collaboration tools.

I = INTEGRATION OF OPERATIONS ON A GLOBAL LEVEL

Of the companies studied in depth here, only 70 percent focused extensively on integrating operations on a global basis. Yet this is not a trivial goal – even the stars of global operations strategy are still not quite sure how best to fully integrate global operations.

Optimize global competencies through partnering. To execute effectively, a global partnering strategy is becoming increasingly important. As Figure 1 shows, 55 percent of CEOs plan to partner as a strategy for global integration. Moreover, when we looked at partnering as a type of business model innovation, we found that more than 40 percent of CEOs we surveyed are changing their enterprise models to be more collaborative, notably via partnering strategies.

And, again, with technology dramatically reducing the costs and challenges of collaborating virtually, more and more companies are using global partnering to enter new markets, reach new customers and team with the best suppliers, manufacturers and others throughout increasingly disaggregated enterprises. That is, what once might have been done within the walls of a company can now be done via partnerships and global supply chains.

ELI LILLY: PARTNERING FOR GLOBAL ADVANTAGE

US pharmaceutical giant Eli Lilly and Company pioneered a "research without walls" approach to R&D in the mid-1990s in order to revive its innovation pipeline, reduce upfront development costs and still accelerate the pace of discovery. To do this, Lilly has integrated an extensive network of external partners in academia, biotech and beyond through its constantly evolving, collaborative business models. The results have been impressive – from 2002 to 2007, sales increased at a compound annual growth rate of 11 percent.

Manage end-to-end processes on a global basis. Bringing all of these approaches together, the final step in global integration is managing on a global basis for every process from end to end, within and beyond company walls. Key to this is a systems view of global operations, with tools and methodologies in place to continually monitor end-to-end processes while adjusting to changes wherever and whenever they arise, while maintaining the focus on global optimization.

IBM: TAKING A GLOBAL VIEW

In recent years, IBM has undergone an extensive, dedicated transformation process to evolve from a multinational company to a truly globally integrated enterprise. As part of this effort, IBM reduced multiple supply chain processes and systems from numerous local procurement centers to just three global procurement centers, contributing to a significant reduction in total supply chain spend. IBM also reduced IT complexity, moving from numerous local CIOs and local data centers to just one global CIO and five global data centers. This has greatly improved efficiency while reducing IT spending as well. Similar efforts have streamlined and integrated operations on a global scale in human resources, finance, marketing, R&D, sales, the leadership structure and other key areas of the company, contributing in part to the company's strong performance even amid the widespread external economic challenges of 2008.

FOUNDATIONS OF R-O-I: LEADERSHIP, ORGANIZATION AND TECHNOLOGY

In concert with the R-O-I elements, three additional elements underpin the global integration transformation process and together serve as the foundation that enables globally integrated operations: leadership; organization; and technology.

Leadership

Integration efforts are most likely to succeed when strong leadership is actively involved in and held accountable for driving required changes throughout the organization. Such leaders set the overall direction of the organization, with clear targets for operationalizing the strategy, and then influence others to commit support to a global integration program.

For example, back in the 1950s when the Toyota leadership realized it had to significantly improve efficiency and cut costs to survive, the Toyota Production System was born – operationalizing this system then followed, evolving and improving over time. Likewise, the recent IBM transformation from multinational to globally integrated enterprise was driven by the CEO and then cascaded throughout the organization to top global leaders.

Integrating operations requires optimizing global competencies via partnering, as well as managing end-to-end processes on a global basis.

Organization

A structured approach to change management is a critical enabling factor for instituting new, globally integrated operations throughout the organization, addressing shifts in roles, responsibilities and relationships. Governance is then essential for ongoing oversight, linking business strategy to operational execution from end to end in all processes and instituting controls over quality and costs while managing risk.

For example, when Eli Lilly and Company launched its "research without walls" initiative, it also set up an Office of Alliance Management to establish a systematic approach to the growing network of external partners, rather than treat each new alliance as a separate relationship. This allowed for continual learning and improvement of the overall approach to partners.

Technology

Finally, technology is at the core of the transformation in enterprise structure, enabling far more collaboration within and across organizations. Geography is a far less limiting factor than in previous eras, certainly much less so than in the pre-Internet age. And as communications technology evolves, maverick business leaders will keep raising the bar for competitors, figuring out ways to leverage technology to do things faster, cheaper, better.

Foundational elements of the R-O-I framework provide critical support, spanning leadership, organizational structure and technology.

With global integration as the goal of many, technology will be key to its enablement: connecting end-to-end processes globally throughout the extended enterprise; removing redundant systems; reducing manual activity; and optimizing operations on a global basis. For example, as described above, Li & Fung relies on sophisticated systems to manage its global network of suppliers, in a pull structure centering on rapid response to demand.

FIGURE 5 **WHILE MANY ORGANIZATIONS MANAGE PROCESSES, ASSETS AND OPERATIONS ON A LOCAL BASIS, THE BEST INTEGRATE THESE GLOBALLY IN AN "R-O-I" FRAMEWORK**

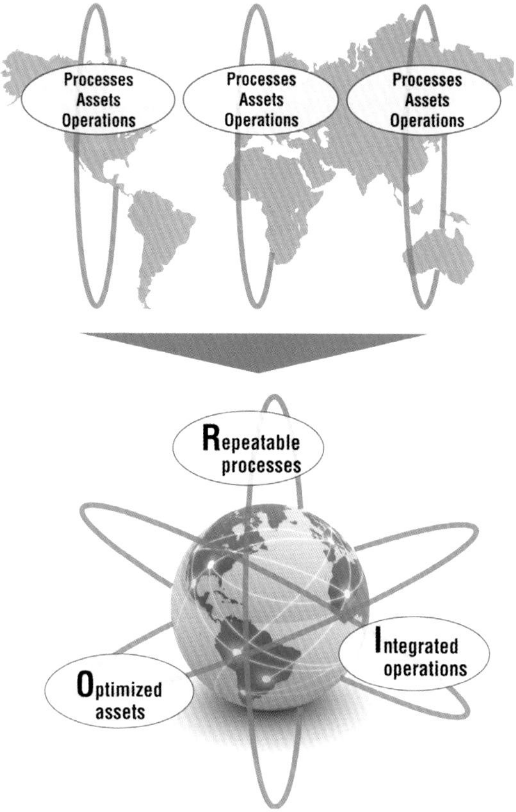

CONCLUSION

The new economic environment has intensified pressures to cut costs and optimize resources and capital productivity. By working toward a fully "globally integrated enterprise," firms can not only achieve these ends, they can also drive growth, in particular enabling entry into new markets.

But an ad hoc or piecemeal approach is not sufficient; in order to achieve truly globally integrated operations, it is essential to address all elements of the R-O-I framework simultaneously and well. And the strongest competitors, especially in the new economic environment, understand that getting this right is an increasingly important competitive differentiator.

ARE YOU READY?

Despite an increasing awareness among CEOs and other business leaders of the importance of global integration, they often stumble when it comes to establishing the operational capabilities needed to support global integration. Many still manage their processes, assets and operations locally. Even those focused on global integration often do so on a piecemeal basis, rather than in a strategic, systemic, comprehensive way. Top performers, however, have a systemic view and are integrating processes, assets and operations on a global basis, see Figure 5.

To help determine your own organization's level of global integration, answer the following questions. This self-assessment can pinpoint areas of weakness so you can give appropriate attention to all areas of the R-O-I framework via a comprehensive approach.

Repeatable processes

How will you eliminate redundancies to support efficient global operations?

How can you optimize the effectiveness of your operations to establish high quality standards while focusing on the areas that really matter to customers?

How are you managing the exceptions to repeatable, standardized processes? Are you keeping exceptions to no more than 20 percent of all transactions?

Optimized assets

How will you identify core versus non-core processes? What is your plan for managing the non-core processes via outsourcing or other solutions?

What will you do to locate processes strategically on a global basis to optimize assets, talent, resources, distance to markets and other key factors of production?

Integrated operations

What is your partnering strategy to optimize global competencies?

How can you manage every process from end to end, within and beyond company walls, on a global basis?

Leadership

Given the scale and scope of global integration efforts, how can your leadership prepare to drive the necessary changes throughout the organization?

Organization

What is your organization's consistent method for change management? What processes and technologies are in place to allow people to become involved in the change, access accurate information and provide feedback?

Can your governance structures continually monitor processes in order to verify consistent quality throughout widespread global locations?

Technology

How will you build the systems and technological infrastructure to support globally integrated operations?

ABOUT THE AUTHORS

Dave Lubowe is a Partner in IBM Global Business Services' Strategy and Change practice and is the Global and Americas Leader for Operations Strategy. He has 25 years of industry and consulting experience, primarily in operations management and finance. His consulting work has focused on designing, implementing, managing and improving business processes, including extensive experience in outsourcing. He holds five US patents. He can be contacted at dave.lubowe@us.ibm.com.

Judith Cipollari brings more than 16 years of financial services industry experience to her role as a Senior Managing Consultant in IBM Global Business Services' Strategy and Change practice. Her primary areas of industry expertise are in institutional trust and custody banking and in property and casualty commercial insurance. She has worked with various clients to provide strategy, process design, post-merger integration of operations, global sourcing initiatives and organizational consulting. She can be contacted at cipollar@us.ibm.com.

Patrick Antoine is an Associate Partner in the Strategy and Change Internal Practice of IBM Global Services. He has more than 10 years of experience in strategy consulting, specializing in business transformation, process design, process re-engineering, organizational analysis and program management. His key areas of focus include: transformation to a globally integrated enterprise; shared services strategy and implementation; and transformation to a solution-based business and operational model. He can be contacted at pantoine@us.ibm.com.

Amy Blitz is a Director at the Innovation Management Exchange. She has led major research initiatives on issues related to strategy, innovation and economic development. Her work has been featured in *Harvard Business Review* and *The Wall Street Journal* and at MSNBC and other major media outlets. She can be contacted at ablitz@alum.mit.com.

CONTRIBUTORS

Many colleagues throughout IBM contributed to this paper. Thanks to Saul Berman, Peter Korsten and Dan Latimore for insights into the overall vision and direction of the study; and to Anubha Jain, Mahesh Ganesan, Madhulika Kamjula, Andrew Statton and Ranjit Kher for contributions throughout the research and analysis. Thanks as well to Ron Frank, Mal Flanagan and team for their insights and expertise regarding the "globally integrated enterprise."

REFERENCES

1   Berman, Saul, Steven Davidson, Sara Longworth and Amy Blitz. "Succeeding in the new economic environment: Focus on value, opportunity, speed." IBM Institute for Business Value. February 2009. http://www-935.ibm.com/services/us/index.wss/ibvstudy/gbs/a1030986?cntxt=a1005266

2   Palmisano, Samuel J. "The Globally Integrated Enterprise." *Foreign Affairs*. Vol 85, No. 3. May-June, 2006.

3   "World Investment Report 1996: Investment, Trade and International Policy Agreements." United Nations. August 1996; "World Investment Report 2008: Transnational Corporations and the Infrastructure Challenge." United Nations. July 2008.

4   "World Investment Report 2006: FDI from Developing and Transition Economies." United Nations. October 2006.

5   Hall, Jessica. "Global M&A falls in 2008." Reuters. December 22, 2008.

6   Ghemawat, Pankaj. *Redefining Global Strategy: Crossing Borders in a World Where Differences Still Matter.* Harvard Business School Press. 2007. He notes that the growing trend toward globalization of production "heralds something new in global strategy – something that changes our understanding of the variety of global strategies open to firms today."

7   IBM Corporation. "The Enterprise of the Future: IBM Global CEO Study 2008." May 2008. http://www.ibm.com/enterpriseofthefuture. Based on availability of financial information, we were able to include 530 companies in our financial analysis. We compared performance on three financial benchmarks: revenue compound annual growth rate (CAGR) 2003-2006; net profit margin CAGR 2003-2006; and absolute profit margin average for 2003-2006. Companies that performed above the average for those in the same industry were tagged outperformers; those below the average were labeled underperformers.

8   Ibid.

9   Ghemawat, Pankaj. Op. cit.

10 McGregor, Jena. "The World's Most Innovative Companies: The Leaders in Nurturing Cultures of Creativity." *BusinessWeek*. May 4, 2007. Various company annual reports; IBM Corporation analysis.

11 IBM Corporation. Op. cit.

12 Spear, Stephen J. and H. Kent Bowen. "Decoding the DNA of the Toyota Production System." *Harvard Business Review*. Sep-Oct, 1999.

13 Manrodt, Karl and Kate Vitasek. "Global Process Standardization: A Case Study." *Journal of Business Logistics*. Vol 25, No 1. 2004.

14 "Outsourcing Pharma R&D to India and China." *Offshore Outsourcing World*. September 5, 2005.

15 IBM Global Business Services. "Global Location Trends: Annual Report October 2008." IBM Plant Location International. http://www-935.ibm.com/services/us/gbs/bus/pdf/gbl03005-usen-00hr.pdf

16 Ibid.

17 Robert Half International. The Telework Coalition. http://www.telcoa.org/id33.htm. Accessed on March 23, 2009.

Insights Strategies for
enabling global integration

More than 1,000 CEOs engaged with IBM in the discussions that
underpin *The Enterprise of the Future*. In a series of follow-up
video interviews conducted for the study by 50 Lessons, the
world's premier multimedia business resource – and in interviews
previously conducted by 50 Lessons – some of the world's top
business leaders speak to the study's key themes.

**William K. Fung, Group Managing Director of Li & Fung Limited,
on the links between globalization and collaboration.**
 In the past 20 to 30 years, most innovation and growth has been related to
the process of globalization. And I think that it's almost natural that if you're
moving out of your comfort zone and your domestic market when you're seeking growth opportunities, then you would collaborate with other players in the
new market.
 For Li & Fung, this is particularly relevant because the whole origin of
our company was based on that type of need. To make a long story short, Li
& Fung is a little over 100 years old. When my grandfather first started the
company in Canton in 1906, his role was to provide
Western buyers, who wanted China-related products,
with things like porcelain, silk, tea and so on. They
were working in an alien environment. Obviously,
there was a need for a local business partner to provide that kind of product. For most business people,
collaboration becomes more and more relevant the
further you operate from a familiar market.
 Given the rate of globalization of the past 20 to 30 years, I believe this
collaborative effort will become more and more prevalent. Companies are off-
shoring production and outsourcing at the same time. I think that the world
is in an era of what I would call radical outsourcing – any function that is not
deemed to be a core competence and strategically essential for your company
is a candidate for outsourcing. If somebody else in those areas can do it better,
faster and cheaper than you, maybe that's the way to go, so that you can focus
your energy on areas that are of strategic importance to you.
 This outsourcing trend, besides the globalization trend, is also going to
contribute to the need for co-operation. Your need for local expertise increases
exponentially if your product range is very wide. If you have a narrow product
base, whether you're a brand or a retailer, perhaps it's easier to control the supply chain with your own operation. But if you're selling everything from lawn
mowers to silk underwear, chances are you need a partner or partners all over

> "Companies are offshoring
> production and outsourcing at
> the same time. If somebody else
> in those areas can do it better,
> faster and cheaper than you,
> maybe that's the way to go."

the world to do this. A lot of people talk about buying direct, but they need an intermediation layer. When somebody says that they buy direct from China, chances are they mean that they buy through their buying office in China; or through somebody like a Li & Fung, an agent in China; or through some intermediary. By the same token, if a factory in India says it sells directly to somebody in America, chances are it is selling to a buying office or to Li & Fung.

This is not just because of the need for expertise on the ground. There's a need to control quality. There's a need to control compliance, which is very important now. There's a need to sort out the numerous suppliers – who the good suppliers are, who the bad suppliers are. There's a whole supply chain that's now offshore. If you're buying apparel, chances are that your fabric is made in country A and it's shipped to country B or another part of country A to be made. It's a very complex supply chain. Li & Fung really made its name by managing these very complex supply chains.

William K. Fung is the Group Managing Director of Li & Fung Limited, one of the largest supply chain management companies. Li & Fung, which is based in Hong Kong, is forecasting turnover of $US20 billion for 2008-10 and a core operating profit of $US1 billion by 2010. Mr Fung is also a Director of various companies with the Li & Fung group of companies, including publicly listed Convenience Retail Asia Limited and Integrated Distribution Services Group Limited.

Ravi Kant, Executive Vice-Chairman and former Managing Director of Tata Motors, on globalization through acquisition.

Ten years ago, we unveiled a three-phase strategy: turning the company around in two years; strengthening our position in the domestic market; and going into the international market. We felt that we already had a high market share in commercial vehicles – more than 60 percent – and we had to protect that market share in this country. So if we wanted to grow, even in terms of passenger cars, we had to go to other countries.

"Our template for international business has been to be seen as a local company."

Two options were available to us. One was organic growth – go from scratch and start working upwards. Surely this is something we had to do, but it would take a long time. The other was inorganic, meaning through mergers and acquisitions. We decided that we should go with both. It is for this reason that our turnover today is close to $US25 billion, an increase of almost ten times in a span of about seven or eight years. That's huge growth, and that has happened because of mergers and acquisitions.

The first part of this happened in Korea. There was a company called Daewoo Truck Company, which was for sale. We were one of ten bidders, and we finally succeeded in getting the company. We have done very well there; both the top and bottom lines have increased substantially. The second event was that we took on a stake in a Spanish bus company with manufacturing locations in Spain and Morocco. The third one – the big one – was Jaguar and Land Rover.

Our template for international business has been to be seen as a local company. For example, we want to be seen as a South Korean company in South Korea. We don't want to be seen as an Indian company in South Korea. Similarly, we want to be seen as a South African company in South Africa and a British company in Britain. What does that mean? It means that you need local management. You need to connect yourself with the local society. You must, therefore, feel the pain and the pleasure of being in that society, and not be seen as an outsider.

That is difficult to implement. In a way, it's a hands-off philosophy. You give responsibility to the local management yet hold them accountable at the same time. That doesn't mean they are free to do anything that they want. There will be a budget, and they'll be responsible for that. We will give a critical analysis. We'll act as a sounding board. We'll act as the facilitators for them to do well. But, ultimately, they have to take the ownership and responsibility.

Ravi Kant is Executive Vice-Chairman and former Managing Director of Tata Motors, India's largest automobile company. In 2007 Tata finalized an agreement to purchase the Jaguar and Land Rover brands from Ford for a reported $US2.3 billion, and in 2008 it unveiled the world's cheapest car, the Nano.

Anders Dahlvig, former Group President and CEO of IKEA, on daring to be different.

Around 1997 we started considering going into Russia in terms of retail operations. In 1998, when we were prepared to start, Russia went into real crisis – political turmoil and economic turmoil. The ruble was going down the drain. There was a lot of uncertainty and a lot of international companies that had been thinking of going into Russia abandoned those plans. Some also left Russia. So there was really no investment flow into Russia.

Part of IKEA's success is that we try to do the opposite of what everyone else is doing. We felt this was a wonderful situation – if we had the courage to move into Russia when everyone else was leaving. It's all about doing things differently to gain a real competitive edge. Of course, we did a little bit of preplanning in the sense of looking at the financial risks. So we said, if we were to invest so many billion euros in new stores in Russia, and everything was lost, confiscated or whatever, what damage would that do to IKEA? We saw that we could have absorbed that without putting the company at risk.

"Part of IKEA's success is that we try to do the opposite of what everyone else is doing."

So we decided to move into Russia. And it was not easy, in the sense that moving into a country in that situation has a lot of problems. There is corruption, bureaucracy and things like that – uncertainties about currencies, financing. On the other hand, it opened up a lot of opportunities to find good sites for our stores and shopping centers. We made the right decision when we put in a crew of people who were really "crazy," in that they would go through walls to accomplish what they needed to do.

Countries like Russia are not easy for a Western company to operate in. But if it was easy, everyone else would have been there as well, and we would not have had the opportunities we did. So for us, the more difficult it is, in some ways, the better. Because if we have the persistence to prevail in this type of environment, it gives us a huge advantage compared with other companies.

Anders Dahlvig was the Group President and CEO of IKEA, a leading international retailer of home furnishing products, for 10 years until September 2009. IKEA offers more than 12,000 products and has 300 stores in 37 countries. From 1998 to 2008, sales grew from 6.3 billion euros to more than 21.2 billion euros.

These insights are drawn from interviews published by Harvard Business Press in Built for Change, *an exclusive edition of the Lessons Learned series and the result of a content partnership between IBM and 50 Lessons.*

Seizing the advantage

When and how to innovate your business model

Edward Giesen, Eric Riddleberger,
Richard Christner and Ragna Bell

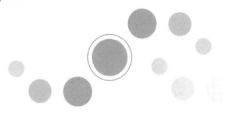

In today's increasingly complex and fast-changing
environment, business model innovation is critical to success.
Yet few understand when to make a change, or – more
importantly – how to execute. Based on a follow-up to *T
he Enterprise of the Future* and an analysis of 28 successful
business model innovators, we gained insight into when
and how to innovate the business model.[1,2] Organizations
can determine the right timing based on the economic
environment, the state of industry transformation and
a set of internal factors that includes the degree of product
and service innovation and the available financial resources.
To increase the chances of success, organizations must build
a set of capabilities we call the Three A's: Organizations need
to be *aligned* with customer value; *analytical* to gain insight
from differentiated intelligence; and enabled by an *adaptable*
operating model.

In *The Enterprise of the Future*, we learned that CEOs expect more turbulent change than ever before. But few would have anticipated the severity and depth of the economic downturn that started in the second half of 2008 and

117

created a new economic environment. *The Enterprise of the Future* showed that financial outperformers are able to leverage change to their advantage. Indeed, they seek to disrupt competitors, redefine industries and increase market share.

So how do companies take advantage of change? CEOs told us that innovating their business model is one of the most prominent strategies. In fact, seven out of ten are pursuing business model innovation to a large extent, and an incredible 98 percent are adapting their business models to some degree (see box below).[3]

THERE IS GROWING AGREEMENT ON THE DEFINING ELEMENTS OF A BUSINESS MODEL [4]

- **What value is delivered to customers**: customer segments, the value proposition, the specific "job to be done," what is sold and how it is sold.
- **How revenue is generated**: the pricing model and forms of monetization.
- **How the company positions itself in the industry**: the company's role and relationships across the value chain.
- **How the value is delivered**: key internal resources and processes, as well as external partnerships.

With unprecedented change upon us and business model innovation becoming pervasive, two questions can help companies develop their strategy and transformation approach for the new economic environment:

- Under what conditions should companies innovate their business model?
- What capabilities and characteristics support the design and execution of successful business model innovation?

This chapter builds on ongoing IBM research into business model innovation and a broad set of data available from our Global CEO Studies to explore these questions. We provide practical guidance to help organizations define their strategic agendas for business model innovation.

WHEN TO INNOVATE YOUR BUSINESS MODEL

Most people think a recession is the time to hunker down and ride out the storm. But they may be wrong. Periods of economic turmoil and transition create significant opportunities to gain advantage. Our research suggests business model innovation can be an effective way to capitalize on those opportunities.[5] Successful timing of business model innovation depends on: the economic environment; the specific market and industry conditions; and a set of internal organizational factors.

Economic conditions

We see successful companies taking advantage of emerging opportunities in the new economic environment by innovating their business model in three ways:

- Many organizations revisit their *enterprise model* during a downturn to reduce cost through new collaboration and partnership models and by reconfiguring the asset mix.
- Industry leaders with strong financial resources take advantage of the unprecedented *industry transformation* by introducing alternative industry models and disrupting their competitors.
- Many also rethink their *revenue model and value propositions* to respond to a different set of customer behaviors and market requirements.

While any type of business model innovation can lead to success, financial outperformers are more likely to be industry and enterprise model innovators than revenue model innovators (see Figure 1). Enterprise model innovation is the most prominent, especially during challenging economic times.

Industry model innovation is less frequent, but is more likely to be pursued by industry leaders with strong financial means and industry positions that can leverage bold moves to expand their leadership. Revenue model innovation is considered easiest, but tends not to yield the same financial benefits, as the innovations are less defendable or lasting.

FIGURE 1 **OUTPERFORMERS ARE MORE LIKELY TO BE INDUSTRY AND ENTERPRISE MODEL INNOVATORS**

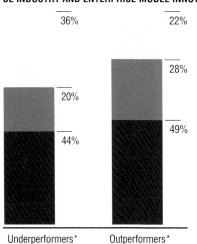

36%   22%

20%

44%

28%

49%

Underperformers*   Outperformers*

Source: IBM Global CEO Study 2008. * Performance based on industry comparisons within survey sample of absolute profit margin (average of 2003 and 2006); n (underperformers) =120, n (outperformers) =109.

Types of business model innovation:

Revenue model innovation
Innovate how the company makes money by changing the value proposition (product/service/value mix) and the pricing model.

Industry model innovation
Redefine an existing industry, move into a new industry or create an entirely new one.

Enterprise model innovation
Innovate the way the organization operates, rethinking the organizational boundaries of what is done in-house and what is done through collaboration and partnering.

Revenue model innovation

■ Industry model innovation

■ Enterprise model innovation

Revisit the enterprise model: Enterprise model innovation is especially prominent during economic downturns as companies seek new ways to gain cost and flexibility advantages (see Figure 2). Enterprise model innovators focus on those areas of the business where they have an advantage and deliver value, and they partner extensively for other areas of their business.

FIGURE 2 **TIMING OF LEADING BUSINESS MODEL INNOVATORS IMPLEMENTING A NEW MODEL**

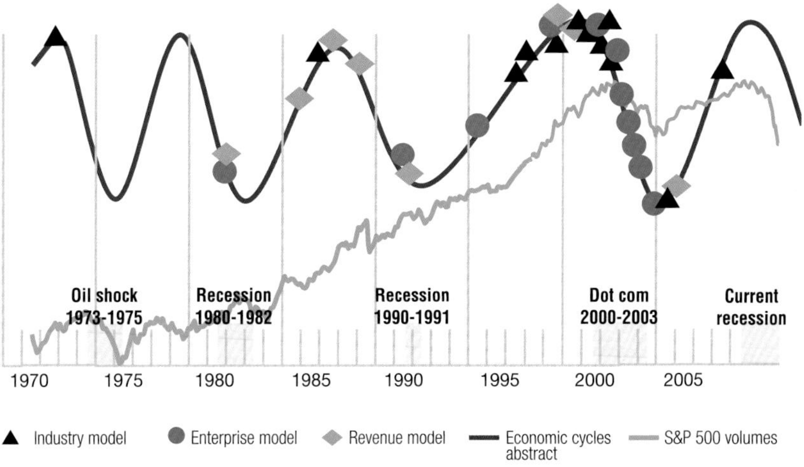

Source: Bureau of Economic Analysis, USA Today, S&P 500, IBM Institute for Business Value analysis.
Note: Representation of specific business model innovations of leading innovators.

While many of the cases portrayed in Figure 2 occurred in prior economic cycles, they illustrate how organizations exploit enterprise model innovation to reduce cost and increase flexibility during a downturn. We clearly see this playing out again now.

Large multinational companies are increasingly interested in outsourcing non-core activities and IT functions to India and China. Local governments are also using outsourcing and technology transformation to radically lower their cost bases. Increased collaboration and partnering are prominent in industries such as pharmaceuticals and biotechnology, in which reduced access to capital and resources is driving the need for new funding and partnership.

Li & Fung is a good example of enterprise model innovation. It is one of the largest producers of fashion, but its core competency is neither fabrics nor design. In contrast to many competitors, Li & Fung turned its focus to orchestrating a complex network of players across the value chain without owning many of the physical assets required for designing, producing and distributing the products. Li & Fung is now taking advantage of the economic environment by making select global acquisitions and continuing to build out its partnership model.[6]

Exploit industry transformation: As seen in Figure 2, industry model innovation is more prominent after long periods of economic expansion, when access to financing is more readily available and companies are willing to take on more risk. However, companies that perform well during the good times and create their own financial resources to innovate their business model can gain the greatest benefit when applying industry model innovation during an economic downturn. They are better positioned to achieve significant margin improvement than companies that don't have the financial resources to make bold moves or simply aren't focused on business model innovation.

A joint IBM-Carnegie Mellon Tepper School of Business study analyzed the 2007 and 2008 financial performance of business model innovators that participated in *The Enterprise of the Future*. This analysis found that the strongest margin performance was realized by those companies that entered the downturn with significant financial means and leveraged their resources to drive industry model innovation.[7]

In the financial services industry, for example, the financial crisis and a new regulatory environment precipitated a radical transformation. Two industry giants, Goldman Sachs and JP Morgan Chase, had the economic strength to use the financial and economic turmoil to their advantage and emerged from the downturn as clear leaders.[8]

In another fast-changing industry, Bharti Airtel, the Indian mobile telecommunications provider, has been able to leverage its financial strength to pursue new industry models. Traditionally known as a strong enterprise model innovator – based on its radical partnering business model – Bharti now leverages its financial strength to explore new industry opportunities. This includes moving into the media and entertainment space, which was ripe for innovation, and exploring ways of providing health and banking services to the "unbanked" millions within India's population.[9]

Develop new value propositions and pricing models to fit customer preferences: Revenue model innovation may not deliver an advantage as sustainable as industry or enterprise model innovation, but in times of economic turmoil new customer preferences and spending patterns are a significant impetus to changing the pricing model and value proposition.

The automotive industry is a good example. While most car manufacturers in the US drastically cut prices in 2008, the Korean manufacturer Hyundai introduced a new pricing model and value proposition with great initial success. Consumers were able to return their cars within the first year and have their debt cancelled. Hyundai's pricing strategy addressed the high degree of uncertainty consumers were feeling, rather than simply cutting prices.[10]

Revenue model innovation has also come to the forefront as access to capital has dwindled and traditional revenue streams have slowed. This has sharpened the focus on a company's ability to realize value not five years out, but within much shorter time horizons. For example, in the media industry, businesses such as online newspapers, which were based primarily on the expectation of future advertising revenues, are being re-evaluated with stronger emphasis on subscription and consumer-pays models.

Industry transformation

During periods of relative stability in the industry landscape, companies can make incremental adjustments to their business model over extended periods of time. They can continue to realize the economic benefits of their existing business model. During periods of extensive industry change, however, companies must choose to shake up their industries – harness disruptive technologies, go after new customer segments, dislodge competitors – or face their own demise (see Figure 3).

FIGURE 3 **BUSINESS MODEL INNOVATION DURING PERIODS OF EXTENSIVE ENVIRONMENTAL CHANGE**

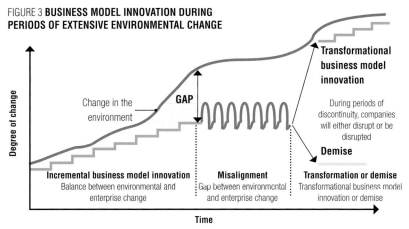

Source: Adapted from Gerry Johnson, Kevan Scholes, Richard Whittington, Exploring Corporate Strategy, 7th Edition © 2005 Prentice Hall, Pearson Education Limited.

In the rapidly evolving video rental and subscription business, for example, technology change and content digitization has transformed the industry, spawning a succession of new business models. Blockbuster has been challenged by fast-growing online competitors with disruptive businesses models such as Netflix. Over the past three years, Blockbuster's response has been gradual adaptation of its business model, adding, for example, a "Total Access" package for receiving DVDs through rental stores or by mail, and announcing a partnership with CinemaNow to deliver movies on demand via the Internet.[12] However, the incremental approach has not been enough to stay ahead of industry transformation and the economic downturn. As a result, Blockbuster is undergoing fundamental restructuring, including the closure of nearly 1,000 video rental stores.[12]

Internal factors

Internally driven changes – such as product or service innovations – can also generate the need for a new business model. In taking them to market, a number of questions need to be addressed. How much does the new product or service change the business model in general and the customer value proposition in particular? Does the existing pricing model need to be adjusted? What about technology, skills and resources and the overall operating model?

Product and service innovation is a key driver for new business models. For example, the development of a high-end instant coffee technology by Nestlé prompted the need for a completely new business model. In fact, it spurred the creation of a separate company in the 1980s, Nespresso, a one-serve coffee product targeted at the high-end consumer market (see sidebar, "Nespresso: Success through internal alignment").

Financial performance and the availability of key resources are both drivers and enablers of business model innovation. In the technology services industry, IBM has a track record of using its financial strength to invest heavily in research and business model transformation during periods of economic downturn. By investing in research and development during the depths of the Great Depression in the 1930s, IBM was ready when the recovery began.[13] Similarly, IBM is today investing heavily in the development of "Smarter Planet" initiatives, based on its view that virtually every process, system and infrastructure can be instrumented, interconnected and infused with intelligence. This opens up entirely new market opportunities for new partnerships and business models.[14]

Is this the right time?

Every organization needs to review carefully whether the time is right to revisit its business model, either to pursue new opportunities in its industry or to respond to competitive or technology threats posed to its existing model. We have developed a structured set of questions to help you understand the conditions in which an organization should explore business model innovation. If a number of these factors apply to you and your industry to a large extent, the right time to revisit your business model is now (see Figure 4).

THE THREE A'S OF BUSINESS MODEL INNOVATION

If the timing is right, how does an organization go about innovating its business model? Established companies have to manage legacy transition issues, which often allow start-ups and new entrants to capture significant value in industries in turmoil. However, our research has shown that new and innovative business models can – and do – succeed regardless of a company's age, industry or geography.

FIGURE 4 **FACTORS DRIVING THE NEED FOR BUSINESS MODEL INNOVATION**

External factors and industry transformation	
Value chain	Have there been shifts in your value chain such as the introduction of "direct" models or value migration along the value chain?
New entrants	Are new market entrants introducing models that would disrupt your industry?
Competitors	Do you see competitors introducing innovative propositions or models impacting your business?
Customer preferences	Are customer preferences for goods, services or channels changing?
Customer segments	Do you see new customer segments emerging that would require delivery of different products, services or delivery through new models?
Technology	Are there disruptive new technologies emerging?
Regulatory/legal	Has there been significant change to your regulatory environment, either by industry or geography, that impacts your current business model?
Environment	Are there social and environment sustainability factors that impact your current model?
Internal factors	
Product/service innovation	Are you taking a new product or service to market that requires a new set of skills, capabilities and processes which leads to a new value proposition and pricing strategy?
Performance	Are you in a period of declining or negative growth relative to your industry?
Resource availability	Are you delivering economic returns that provide the financial resources to make bold moves? Can you leverage the right skills and capabilities?

Source: IBM Institute for Business Value.

We reviewed 28 cases of recognized innovators, as well as select organizations that either tried to innovate their business models and failed or simply missed the window of opportunity.[15] Based on this analysis, we identified a set of characteristics that strong business model innovators demonstrate consistently (see Figure 5).

These characteristics – the "Three A's" – are critical to the successful design and execution of business model innovation:

- **Aligned** – Leverage core capabilities and enforce consistency across all dimensions of the business model, internally and externally, that build customer value;
- **Analytical** – Use information strategically to create foresight, and prioritize actions while measuring and tracking for rapid course correction;
- **Adaptable** – Link innovative leadership with the ability to effect change and create operating model flexibility.

FIGURE 5 **THE "THREE A'S" MODEL FOR BUSINESS MODEL INNOVATION**

Source: IBM Institute for Business Value.

We found that each of the Three A's is important for successful and sustainable business model innovation. Strong business model innovators often combine all three characteristics and realize the associated value. For example, on a scale of 1 to 3, we found that successful business model innovators had an average score of 2.6 for the *Aligned* characteristic, compared with an average score of just 1.3 for those who were not successful at innovating their business model (see Figure 6).

FIGURE 6 **STRONG BUSINESS MODEL INNOVATORS DEMONSTRATE THE THREE A'S**

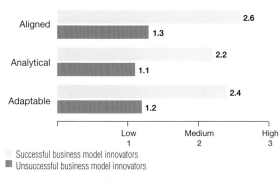

Source: IBM Institute for Business Value analysis. Successful business model innovators n=28.
Unsuccessful business model innovators n=11.

Aligned: Creating internal and external consistency

When looking at the dimensions that shape business model innovation, there is growing agreement that these dimensions have to be fully aligned.[16] Internally, this requires that organizations start with the customer value proposition and align all dimensions of the organization, including the ways in which revenue is generated and value delivered. Externally, organizations need to orchestrate a network of customers, partners and suppliers through open collaboration and partnership models. Finally, many successful business model innovators leverage existing assets and capabilities in new and unique ways.

Align internally to provide customer value: While each business model element is critical in its own right, the success of business model innovation depends on their consistent alignment with each other. Understanding how the elements of business model innovation relate, and how they create value, is critical as an organization goes through the process of adapting or changing its business model. The importance of alignment became evident when we compared successful business model innovations against those that failed.

Take the airline industry, for example. Carriers such as Southwest Airlines and Ryanair revolutionalized the industry at the low end by introducing an innovative value proposition consisting of low-cost, point-to-point air travel supported by strong customer service. To deliver this model, Ryanair, for example, aligned all aspects of its organization and operations to be low-cost, including standardizing its fleet of aircraft to minimize repair and maintenance cost while increasing bargaining power with suppliers, choosing secondary airports with lower airport fees and disaggregating the pricing model so that it charges customers for all extras.

In contrast, several established carriers that introduced low-cost subsidiaries tried to deliver the same low-cost proposition within their high-cost operating models, including operations and processes, systems and people. These models were largely unsuccessful and typically failed within a few years.[17]

Align externally with partners through "open" business models: External alignment with partners, suppliers and customers through open, collaborative business models is an important characteristic of effective business model innovation. Seven out of ten CEOs surveyed for *The Enterprise of the Future* focus on collaboration and partnerships in their pursuit of business model innovation.[18] A number of open business models are largely built on broad collaboration and partnering, such as Li & Fung's global production model, Eli Lilly's spun-off "InnoCentive" model or the Linux operating system. However, our research shows that virtually every successful business model demonstrates external alignment and the ability to orchestrate a large number of collaboration partners.

NESPRESSO: SUCCESS
THROUGH INTERNAL ALIGNMENT

Nestlé's Nespresso single-serve premium coffee business is a good example of how internal alignment to the value proposition is critical to delivering success. Based on its product innovation of a single-pod espresso system, Nestlé explored various ways of commercializing the new system in the 1980s. After unsuccessful attempts to penetrate the restaurant and office market, Nespresso was set up as a wholly owned subsidiary in 1986 and started to align its business model elements with delivering the high-quality coffee experience to the high-income home.

Given the extent of differences between Nespresso Café and other Nestlé coffee brands (for example, Nescafé instant coffee), this required a complete departure from Nestlé's traditional model. The success of Nespresso was largely linked to the ability to create a separate, internally aligned, business model with independent leadership – serving a distinct customer segment (high-end households versus the traditional mass market) through new distribution channels (mail and Internet order and luxury stores versus traditional mass retail), with different brand positioning (high-end luxury brand versus traditional mass-market branding) and a new set of external partnerships, including coffee machine manufacturers who independently distribute their machines and retain the profit.

The Nespresso model has proved successful and defendable. Nespresso achieved 35 percent annual growth over the past decade, and even during 2008, at the height of the economic crisis, it achieved 30 percent year-on-year revenue growth.[19]

Use existing assets and capabilities: Successful business model innovation takes advantage of existing assets and capabilities within the organization, such as unique skills, talent, processes or technology. Apple, for example, leveraged the ability to effectively design user experiences and applied it to the music industry when designing and launching the iPod.

Are you aligned?
- How does your organization ensure internal alignment of your customer value proposition and all aspects of the organization, including the pricing model, the operating model, the role you play in your industry and its talent?
- Does your organization optimize external partnerships and collaboration as part of your business model?
- Does your organization leverage unique existing assets as you design and execute new business models?

TATA MOTORS ALIGNS WITH PARTNERS TO DELIVER NANO

Tata Motors' new Nano is based on the premise of delivering an affordable car for Indian families. In order to deliver this value proposition at a revolutionary price point of $US2,500, Tata Motors had to align its entire organization, supply chain and channels. To deliver a viable model, it had to reconfigure how a car was designed, manufactured and distributed. It redefined its supplier strategy, choosing to outsource a remarkable 85 percent of the Nano's components and to use nearly 60 percent fewer vendors than normal to reduce transaction costs. Tata also brought in key suppliers early in the design phase and challenged them to act as partners in bringing costs down in unprecedented ways.[20]

Analytical: Leveraging business intelligence for greater insight

Successful business model innovators demonstrate a particularly acute understanding of their customers and the value that their company can deliver to a new segment, through a new delivery mechanism or with a new product or service "wrapped" in a new business model. Increasingly, understanding customers, markets, channels and competitors is based on better information. This is then used to create advantage in new and unique ways. Successful innovators use large amounts of data coming from inside and outside the enterprise to:

- Create the strategic foresight needed to design the business models of the future;
- Understand their potential economic impact;
- Continuously measure and enhance performance.

Strategic foresight: Foresight is critical if organizations are to understand new opportunities and the potential impact of new technologies, emerging customer segments or a new set of product or service capabilities. For example, the insurance company Progressive has built advanced customer and risk analytics into its business model, allowing it to serve a higher-risk customer segment profitably. Li & Fung has built analytics and foresight into its strategic process. In the company's words, it uses foresight and planning to "institutionalize the process of reinvention."[20]

The ability to better understand potential future scenarios and how the organization can benefit through new models is more important than ever before as organizations have to operate – and make decisions – in a more complex and rapidly changing environment.

Financial business modeling: Financial business modeling provides the ability to simulate the interaction (and therefore the financial impact) of different external scenarios and internal changes based on the specific business model innovation. Netflix, the video rental business, has used advanced analytics modeling effectively to support pricing and purchasing decisions (see sidebar, "Netflix: Using analytics for intelligence and insight").

Effectiveness measurements: Well-designed measurements provide timely insight about what is and is not working, better enabling an organization to adapt quickly to new business realities. The ability to sense and respond to change – within the organization and in the external marketplace – is critical. Internally, this requires organizations to integrate fragmented data and perform faster, with better extraction and analysis to support business decisions. Externally, it means that organizations must be able to integrate data across a vast array of partners, suppliers and customers in order to make quick business decisions.

NETFLIX: USING ANALYTICS FOR INTELLIGENCE AND INSIGHT

The video rental business Netflix has built advanced analytics into its business model and continuously leverages insight and analytics to create advantage. The Netflix recommendations engine, for example, is instrumental in helping consumers make rental decisions. Based on user ratings, Netflix "crunches" consumers' rental histories and film ratings to predict what else they'll like. Today, more than half of consumers' video rental queues are generated through advanced analytic algorithms. Building on its recommendation engine, Netflix has also been able to drive the so-called long tail of video rental, with only 30 percent of its movie rentals coming from new releases, compared with 70 percent for Blockbuster.

Netflix also uses data mining and analytics to make pricing decisions in purchasing hard-to-market movies from studios.[22] Since launching its online mail-order video rental in 1999, the number of Netflix subscribers has grown at a compound annual rate of 64 percent, reaching an estimated 9.4 million subscribers at the end of 2008.[23]

Does your business model leverage analytics for intelligence and insight?

- Do you regularly assess the strategic opportunities in your environment, based on new and disruptive models emerging in your industry?
- How detailed and accurate is your customer, supplier and partner information?
- Do you deeply understand what your customers want or how they value your current offerings?
- Does your organization have the means to understand the financial and business impact of different business model options?
- Are you able to assess information in real time, internally and externally, to allow dynamic course correction?

Adaptable: Building flexibility into the business model

Business model adaptability is becoming more important in the new economic environment. We found that successful business model innovators are able to mimic the speed, flexibility and mindset of start-up companies, which account for some of the most radical business model innovations, while exploiting the advantage of existing capabilities, resources and assets. When reviewing both start-ups and established companies, we found that business model adaptability was based on the effective combination of leadership and change capabilities throughout the organization, as well as an operating model that enables dynamic course correction and rapid execution (see sidebar, "Bharti has built adaptability into its business model").

Leadership and change: Successful business model innovators are capable and willing when it comes to pursuing new opportunities and models while maintaining a ruthless focus on sustaining their current business. Often referred to as *ambidexterity*, successful business model innovators are able to explore, experiment and pilot new models without putting the performance of existing models at risk.[24]

For some new business models, this may require separate organizational structures (as Nestlé's Nespresso business did). For others, such as Apple's iPod, it may require organizational unity, with existing models supporting and reinforcing each other. Leaders will need to exhibit the following characteristics:

- **Innovative leadership** – Focused innovation leadership and a willingness to break with the status quo are key aspects of managing for the new while maintaining the old. This includes a willingness to explore breakthrough innovations that challenge the existing business. Strong leadership and perseverance help overcome inherent organizational inertia.
- **Enabling breakthrough innovation** – In addition to innovative leadership, breakthrough innovation requires a culture of innovation and an entrepreneurial mindset. Well-known innovators such as Google and Apple constantly reinvigorate entrepreneurial spirit within their organizations. For example, Apple started flying a pirate flag from its headquarters as a symbol of maintaining a "rebel spirit."
- **Dynamic course correction** – In today's fast-paced environment, dynamic course correction is required to bring new business models to market. Business models can be designed on the "drawing board," but only application and testing in the market – often in the form of piloting – provide the insight needed to understand if and how the business model will succeed. This requires the flexibility to respond quickly to signals from the external environment, economic results and partnership alignment. It involves constantly reviewing what is working and what is not, and adapting key aspects of the model accordingly, especially in fast-moving industries such as the media industry. For example, Netflix continues to adapt its business model based on new technologies, such as adding online

video to its subscription model based on changes in streaming technology capabilities and customer preferences.

Operating model flexibility: A flexible operating model entails four elements.

- **Lean and transparent processes** – In an increasingly complex environment, process optimization and end-to-end process visibility are required to build flexibility and change capabilities. Lean Six Sigma approaches, for example, build the elements of continuous improvement into the operational process, allowing the organization to change or adapt the model based on new business model requirements.
- **Flexible and scalable technology** – While technology innovation often enables – or even creates – new business models, flexibility in the underlying infrastructure is critical in allowing an organization to adapt its business model and to deliver a platform for rapid growth and scaling.
- **Globally optimized operations** – This requires processes that are replicable and repeatable across different geographies, assets that are optimized based on a clear distinction of what is core and what is non-core, the ability to manage processes end to end and extensive partnering.[25] Most importantly, global integration provides organizations with access to the right skills at the right cost at the right time, which supports the successful delivery of business model innovation.
- **Asset and cost flexibility** – Shifting from fixed to variable assets enables faster response to changes in market conditions. This requires a clear understanding of and focus on core activities, with a willingness to partner and collaborate for non-core activities.

BHARTI HAS BUILT ADAPTABILITY INTO ITS BUSINESS MODEL

Bharti Airtel is one of India's largest telecommunications providers, yet it doesn't own a network. It asked the question, "What do customers really value?" The answer: multiple new and innovative services delivered quickly, plus excellent service. Bharti is delivering on that proposition and outmaneuvering its competitors by unshackling itself from investment and management of either the network or the supporting infrastructure.

What Bharti put in place was a global partnering model by outsourcing its network management, IT infrastructure and distribution. This allowed Bharti to pull in expertise from around the globe to give it a fast start in capitalizing on the market opportunity, controlling capital expenditures as its subscriber base ballooned and keeping operational costs down. At the same time, Bharti was very clear about its core focus in five areas: customer management; brand management; people management and motivation; financing; and regulation.[26]

Bharti has grown its subscriber base to more than 100 million subscribers in 2009.[27] Even at the height of the economic crisis in 2008, Bharti was able to grow revenue by 37 percent, with net income up 26 percent.[28] Bharti is now leveraging its financial strength to explore expansion into new markets such as media and entertainment, financial services and health care.

Is your business model adaptable?

- Does your organization have a leadership and change model that allows you to pursue new business opportunities while continuing to focus on your current business?
- Is your operating model flexible enough to shift quickly based on new customer and market opportunities?

CONCLUSION

The new economic environment is pushing many companies to revisit their business model. Each organization needs to consider the potential benefits and hurdles carefully. If the conditions are right to act, success depends on a clear strategy for timing, designing and executing business model innovation. To execute business model innovation effectively, the Three A's are essential organizational capabilities: Companies must be *aligned* with customer value and business model innovation dimensions, *analytical* to provide differentiated intelligence and insight and enabled by an *adaptable* operating model.

Not every company will elect to innovate its business model at the present time. However, building the capabilities now to support future innovation will help position organizations to seize competitive advantage and achieve optimal performance. In doing so, they put themselves in the running to become successful business model innovators and industry leaders.

ABOUT THE AUTHORS

Edward Giesen is a Partner in IBM Global Business Services and leads the Business Strategy practice across Europe, Middle East and Africa. He leads the IBM Strategy and Change practice in Belgium, Luxembourg and The Netherlands, and globally heads the IBM Component Business Modeling community. He has more than 15 years' experience in advising senior clients and has published extensively on the topic of business model innovation. He can be reached at edward.giesen@nl.ibm.com.

Eric Riddleberger is a Partner with IBM Global Business Services and leads the Global Business Strategy practice, as well as the Strategy and Transformation practice in the communications sector. He has more than 25 years of experience in strategy and technology throughout the world with IBM, Booz Allen Hamilton, UBS Capital and AT&T. His work with clients includes corporate transformation, market analysis, strategic planning, mergers and acquisitions and business development. He can be reached at eriddle@us.ibm.com.

Richard Christner is a Partner in the Internal Strategy and Transformation practice within IBM Global Business Services. He has more than 15 years of strategy consulting experience with IBM, Dean & Company and Oliver Wyman/Mercer Management Consulting. He has helped firms develop new and innovative business models in a variety of industries, including technology, transportation, consumer goods, retail and industrial products. He can be reached at christnr@us.ibm.com.

Ragna Bell is the Global Strategy and Change lead for the IBM Institute for Business Value within IBM Global Business Services. She has more than ten years of consulting experience with leading clients, focusing on mergers and acquisitions, customer segmentation, market analysis and corporate transformation. She has co-authored articles on business model innovation and is the Global Program Director for IBM's 2010 Global CEO Study. She can be reached at ragna.bell@us.ibm.com.

EXECUTIVE SPONSORS

Saul Berman, IBM Global Business Services, Global Strategy and Change Leader; Sara Longworth, IBM Global Business Services, North East Europe Strategy and Change Leader.

CONTRIBUTORS

This research would not have been possible without the substantial contributions of the IBM Strategy and Change team, notably Kathleen Scheirle who led the case study development and analyses; Andreas Lindermeier, Giuseppe Bruni, Marc Faeh and Daniel Aronson for their guidance and industry insights; and Sankalp Kumar and Akash Singla for their case study and research support. This research also relied deeply on analysis and insights from our collaboration with the Carnegie Mellon University Tepper School of Business, in particular the research guidance from Bosch Professor of Operations Management Sunder Kekre, statistical analysis by Tat Koon Koh and insights and guidance from Abhay Mishra and Eric Walden.

REFERENCES

1   IBM Corporation. "The Enterprise of the Future: IBM Global CEO Study." May 2008. http://www-935.ibm.com/services/us/gbs/bus/html/gbs-ceo-study-implications.html. In a follow-up to the CEO study, a joint team from the Carnegie Mellon Tepper School of Business and IBM analyzed the 2007 and 2008 financial performance (revenue growth and operating margin expansion) of 194 business model innovators participating in the original study, for which a complete set of data was available.

2   The 28 best-practice cases were selected based on two key sources. We revisited the *BusinessWeek* listing of the most innovative companies in the context of their performance in the 2008 economic turmoil. "The World's Most Innovative Companies." *BusinessWeek*. April 24, 2006. http://www.businessweek.com/magazine/content/06_17/b3981401.htm. We then added strong business model innovators that were top performers during the economic downturn of 2008-2009. See Berman, Saul, Steven Davidson, Sara Longworth and Amy Blitz. "Succeeding in the new economic environment: Focus on value, opportunity and speed." IBM Corporation. 2009.

3   IBM Corporation. Op. cit.

4   The literature on business model innovation is increasingly aligned on definitions and core dimensions. See, for example: Osterwalder, A., and Y. Pigneur. *Business Model Generation*. Self-published. 2009; Johnson, Mark W., Clayton M. Christensen and Henning Kagermann. "Reinventing Your Business Model." *Harvard Business Review*. December 2008.

5   Berman, Saul, Steven Davidson, Sara Longworth and Amy Blitz. "Succeeding in the new economic environment: Focus on value, opportunity and speed." IBM Corporation. 2009.

6   Li & Fung acquisitions during the economic downturn include Wear Me Apparel in the US and the Miles Fashion Group in Germany. Inman, Daniel. "Li & Fung Buys Wear Me Apparel for up to $402 million." FinanceAsia.com. October 21, 2009. http://www.financeasia.com/article.aspx?CIaNID=115106

7   IBM Corporation. See footnote 1.

8   Bowly, Graham. "Two Giants Emerge from Wall Street Ruins." *The New York Times*. July 16, 2009. http://www.nytimes.com/2009/07/17/business/global/17bank.html?_r=1

9   "Bharti Airtel Plans Health Services on Mobile Phones." *The Hindu Business Line*. September 1, 2009. http://www.thehindubusinessline.com/2009/09/01/stories/2009090151500400.htm

10   Colvin, Geoff. *The Upside of the Downturn: Ten Management Strategies to Prevail in the Recession and Thrive in the Aftermath*. Portfolio. 2009. Hyundai also introduced a five-year warranty model and was able to boost sales for August 2009 by 47 percent over the previous year, as many US car manufacturers continued to struggle.

11   De la Merced, Michael J. "Blockbuster Hires Help to Restructure its Debt." *The New York Times*. March 3, 2009. http://www.nytimes.com/2009/03/04/business/media/04blockbuster.html

12   CBS News. "Blockbuster Will Close up to 960 Stores." September 15, 2009. http://www.cbsnews.com/stories/2009/09/15/business/main5313438.shtml

13   "IBM Archives: 1930s." http://www-03.ibm.com/ibm/history/history/decade_1930.html

14 Bramante, Jim, Ron Frank and Jim Dolan. "IBM – Delivering performance through continuous transformation." IBM Corporation. September 2009.

15 For selection of business model innovators, see footnote 2. For a set of "counter-pairs," we analyzed companies that pursued business model innovation with limited success and compared them to strong innovators.

16 See footnote 4.

17 Maynard, Micheline. "More Cuts as United Grounds Its Low-Cost Carrier." *The New York Times*. June 5, 2008. http://www.nytimes.com/2008/06/05/business/05air.html

18 IBM Corporation. "The Enterprise of the Future: IBM Global CEO Study 2008." May 2008. http://www-935.ibm.com/services/us/gbs/bus/html/gbs-ceo-study-implications.html.

19 Saltmarsh, Matthew. "The Sweet Smell of Success at Nestlé." *The New York Times*. February 19, 2009. http://www.nytimes.com/2009/02/19/business/worldbusiness/19iht-nestle.4.20317285.html.
Nestlé does not publish Nespresso profit separately, but provides revenue and revenue growth information. Nestlé press information: "The Avenches Milestone in the Nespresso Success Story." http://www.nestle.com/Resource.axd?Id=CF489C89-60D4-4A6E-8590-091D6D5E0672

20 Johnson, Mark W., Clayton M. Christensen and Henning Kagermann. Op. cit.

21 Interview with William K. Fung, Group Managing Director, Li & Fung Ltd. IBM and 50 Lessons. 2009. http://wwwpreview20-935.events.ibm.com/services/us/gbs/bus/html/gbs-built-for-change.html

22 Mullaney, Timothy. "Netflix – The Mail-order Movie House that Clobbered Blockbuster." *BusinessWeek*. May 25, 2006. http://www.businessweek.com/smallbiz/content/may2006/sb20060525_268860.htm

23 Netflix website. http://ir.netflix.com/

24 O'Reilly, Charles, and Michael Tushman. "Ambidexterity as a Dynamic Capability: Resolving the Innovator's Dilemma." *Research in Organizational Behavior*. Vol 28 (2008): pp. 185-206. (Also Harvard Business School Working Paper, No. 07-088, 2007.)

25 Lubowe, Dave, Judith Cipollari, Patrick Antoine and Amy Blitz. "The R-O-I of globally integrated operations: Strategies for enabling global integration." IBM Corporation. 2009.

26 Interview with Manoj Kohli, Chief Executive Officer and Managing Director, Bharti Airtel Limited. IBM and 50 Lessons. 2009. http://wwwpreview20-935.events.ibm.com/services/us/gbs/bus/html/gbs-built-for-change.html

27 Leahy, Joe. "Bharti Boosts Rural Indian Subscriber Base." *Financial Times*. July 23, 2009. http://www.ft.com/cms/s/0/78de7afc-77ac-11de-9713-00144feabdc0.html

28 Bharti website. http://www.bharti.com/136.html?&tx_ttnews%5Btt_news%5D=317&tx_ttnews%5BbackPid%5D=116&cHash=c9cb9d3479

Insights Seizing the advantage through business model innovation

More than 1,000 CEOs engaged with IBM in the discussions that underpin *The Enterprise of the Future*. In a series of follow-up video interviews conducted for the study by 50 Lessons, the world's premier multimedia business resource – and in interviews previously conducted by 50 Lessons – some of the world's top business leaders speak to the study's key themes.

Manoj Kohli, Chief Executive Officer and Managing Director of Bharti Airtel, on business model reinvention.

When we started our journey in the sector in 1995, we knew that we needed deep pockets for this industry. The telecom sector demands a huge amount of funding – billions and billions of dollars. We also knew that Indian customers would need to be serviced with very affordable prices. Now, these two things actually didn't connect with each other. On one hand, we invest billions of dollars. On the other hand, we sell at a very low price. Obviously, we may not have a viable business plan.

So we thought to ourselves, how do we get over this? We knew that if we were to succeed in this sector, then we had to create a new paradigm, a new business model. On December 6, 2002, we had a meeting in Jaipur during which we decided that if we had to offer the lowest prices in the world, then we needed to have the lowest costs in the world. There was no choice. It was a necessity. So we said, okay, let's now modify the business model according to the needs of the customer. And we asked, what do we do? We initiated a huge, five-part outsourcing strategy.

First, we outsourced our entire network to Ericsson and Nokia. We buy capacity from them not in terms of black boxes but in terms of erlangs, which is the measurement of traffic. So we buy capacity. And we make the payments to them when we utilize that capacity. This was completely innovative and it took about six to eight months to convince the senior management at Ericsson and Nokia, especially their CFOs. Their CFOs are tough, you know. Today our networks do 1.5 billion minutes a day, which is one of the highest in the world. It's been victorious.

> "We knew that if we were to succeed in this sector, then we had to create a new paradigm, a new business model."

Second, we outsourced IT. We knew IT was something that we didn't understand. We are not an IT company; we are a consumer company. So we outsourced IT to IBM and IBM, being the biggest IT company in the world, committed to it. Today, IBM deploys hardware, software, services and people, and they take a percentage of my top line.

The third outsourcing initiative we took on was the call centers. We have 82 million customers, and even if half the customers make one call each a month, we have 41 million calls each month. How do we cope with it? We aren't call center experts. We went to the world's best call centers – fortunately, those [business process outsourcing] companies are in India – and we outsourced to them.

The fourth outsourcing initiative was our tower companies. We build passive infrastructure. We have about 80,000 to 85,000 towers in the country, and we'll build many more in future. So we thought, why don't we share this infrastructure, rather than having every operator build a separate tower for itself, investing so much steel, cement and so on? Why don't we have three operators on the same tower and share the cost? We hived off tower companies, and we have two of the largest tower companies in the world with us now. We are sharing with companies such as Vodafone, Idea and many others in the country.

The fifth outsourcing was on the distribution side. We knew we couldn't develop distribution in India. For example, today we cover 5,000 towns and 400,000 villages, and we can't establish showrooms and shops in all of them. So we said, let's outsource to local entrepreneurs, guys who know the local people and who have the entrepreneurial spirit to carry the Airtel brand. This venture was very successful. Today we have about 900 exclusive Airtel showrooms and we have one million non-exclusive retail outlets. They sell soaps, shampoos and so many other things, but they also sell Airtel.

Overall, what we have done in this new business model is outsource expertise to people who are better than us. And we don't mind saying that. We have kept to ourselves our core competencies, such as customer management. And brand is so important for us – we don't outsource that. People management and motivation of our people, that's our job, too. Financing is our job. And, finally, regulation management is our job. These five things we do because they are our core competencies. Everything else, we don't do. Everything else is done by our strategic partners, who have better domain knowledge, skills and capabilities. Today in the global telecom sector, the Bharti Airtel business model is seen as the most unique, the most viable and great for all emerging markets.

Manoj Kohli is the CEO of Bharti Airtel, a leading integrated telecom company in India. Mr Kohli joined Bharti in 2002 as head of the mobile services unit. As CEO and Joint Managing Director, he heads the integrated telco, which includes mobile services, telemedia services, enterprise services and international operations.

Paul Skinner, former Chairman of Rio Tinto, on the importance of monitoring your business environment to anticipate change.

It's important for any organization to maintain an appropriate level of external focus by continuously scanning the business environment, thinking about changes that might take place and being ready to respond to them with well-developed plans that are properly executed.

I remember – and I go back quite a long way, to the mid-1980s – when I was responsible for managing the Shell business in New Zealand. At this time the country was undergoing fundamental economic change and restructuring. For many years New Zealand had been a highly regulated economy protected by tariffs, lots of internal rules and regulations and subsidies. The country was building up significant levels of foreign debt, and it had reached a point where all this was becoming rather unsustainable. The new government arrived and decided that it would embark upon a major program of economic deregulation. This led to the rapid dismantling of all these controls and significantly changed the business environment for many industries in that country.

I was in the oil refining and marketing business in New Zealand at the time. It, like many other industries, had been highly regulated. There were prescribed rates of return and margins on different phases of the business. As a major player, we were not allowed to own retail outlets, for example, so we were operating within a tightly defined framework, which was really quite limit-

> "You'd better keep monitoring the business environment in which you operate. Be ready to reinvent your business as the opportunities arrive."

ing. As the deregulation flowed through the economy, all of that disappeared very quickly. We were allowed to own retail outlets, we could set our own prices and we could invest where we wanted and reshape our retail network accordingly.

We had been thinking about this at Shell for a long time. We had been tracking the thoughts and opinions of the country's different political parties about our industry, and we were constantly thinking on a scenario basis of how it might change. As a result we'd had a contingency plan in place for some time to deal with the deregulation of our industry. As soon as the political winds started to change direction, we were able to activate that plan and significantly strengthen our position in the market. This came as a result of a very rapid roll-out and execution of our deregulation plan, for which we had already agreed an appropriate level of funding with our shareholders in Europe.

We were able to move much faster than most of our competitors as those changes came about. The major lesson from all this for me was that you'd better keep monitoring the business environment in which you operate. Be ready to reinvent your business as the opportunities arrive and be able to execute well. I think we were able to do that, but it was really dependent upon continuous reappraisal of how our business environment might change.

Paul Skinner was Chairman from 2003 until April 2009 of Rio Tinto, the global mining and minerals company dual-listed in the United Kingdom and Australia. Rio Tinto mines iron, copper, uranium, industrial minerals, gold and diamonds, and also produces aluminum products.

Ravi Kant, Executive Vice-Chairman and former Managing Director of Tata Motors, on innovating to disrupt an industry.

The Nano was created when our Chairman, Mr Ratan Tata, observed that many Indian people and families used two-wheelers for transportation.

A common sight in India is an entire family traveling on a two-wheeler: a husband sitting on the seat, a child standing in front and the wife sitting at the back with a child in her lap. Now, I'm sure you'll understand this is a very unsafe and uncomfortable way of traveling.

At that time he observed that most Indians did not have access to four-wheelers, with between eight and nine million two-wheelers sold in India each year. He saw an opportunity to create a four-wheeler that would be economically accessible to a large number of people and would give them additional safety and comfort.

Shortly thereafter, at a press meeting in Geneva, a reporter asked Mr Tata about the price of this vehicle. At that point in time, two-wheelers were around 40,000 rupees and the cheapest four-wheeler was 200,000 rupees. Mr Tata said 100,000 rupees, which in Indian terminology is one lakh. And since then, this price has stuck. The Nano will cost one lakh, or $US2,500. When we unveiled the Nano in January of 2008, the promise of this price shocked people. Nobody expected that a vehicle could ever be produced at this price.

> "Dream a dream. You have to start from there. And don't think that anything is impossible."

The Nano is very attractive, very comfortable, very nice to drive and tremendously fuel-efficient at 50 miles per gallon – all of the ingredients desired by a customer. The market presented a great opportunity. The Indian middle class is about 400 million people – people who never thought that they would be able to ride a four-wheeler. Suddenly, they find that they can reach that goal; they can do it. It has brought about a huge groundswell of interest.

The key lesson that I would like to share is: Dream a dream. You have to start from there. And don't think that anything is impossible, because in this case we didn't go about trying to upgrade a two-wheeler or downgrade a passenger car. We took a plain sheet of paper, started working, and said, "Okay, if the price is going to be this, then the total cost of the vehicle has to be that." We then broke down these costs into various components and aggregates. That's how we began to start working and how we began talking with all of our suppliers. I must say that a lot of suppliers didn't think it was possible at that price, but they looked at the entire concept and came up with a fantastically innovative solution. And it's the combination of all of these things that has made the Nano possible.

Ravi Kant is Executive Vice-Chairman and former Managing Director of Tata Motors, India's largest automobile company. In 2007 Tata finalized an agreement to purchase the Jaguar and Land Rover brands from Ford for a reported $US2.3 billion, and in 2008 it unveiled the world's cheapest car, the Nano.

These insights are drawn from interviews published by Harvard Business Press in Built for Change, *an exclusive edition of the Lessons Learned series and the result of a content partnership between IBM and 50 Lessons.*

Leading a sustainable enterprise
Leveraging insight and information to act

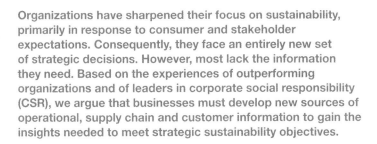

Eric Riddleberger
and Jeffrey Hittner

Organizations have sharpened their focus on sustainability,
primarily in response to consumer and stakeholder
expectations. Consequently, they face an entirely new set
of strategic decisions. However, most lack the information
they need. Based on the experiences of outperforming
organizations and of leaders in corporate social responsibility
(CSR), we argue that businesses must develop new sources of
operational, supply chain and customer information to gain the
insights needed to meet strategic sustainability objectives.

Today, more than ever, organizations are focused on environmental and
social responsibility as a strategic objective. Our 2009 survey of 224 business leaders worldwide shows that 60 percent believe CSR has increased in
importance over the past year (see Figure 1).[1] Only 6 percent say it has become
a lower priority. These responses defy the conventional wisdom that the new
economic environment dilutes CSR focus.

The conditions of a faster, flatter and more interconnected world are without question changing business strategy, as is a greater awareness of systemic
risk and its consequences. These same conditions make a strong case for a
sustainable approach to doing business, one that recognizes that the long-
term health of an organization is inextricably tied to the well-being of society
and the planet on which we live.

FIGURE 1 **CHANGE IN IMPORTANCE OF CSR TO STRATEGIC OBJECTIVES OVER THE PAST YEAR**

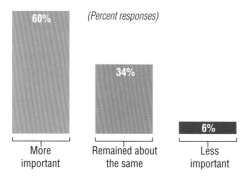

(Percent responses)

60%

34%

6%

More important   Remained about the same   Less important

Source: IBM Institute for Business Value 2009 CSR Study.

To be sustainable, businesses are now embracing a relatively new objective: optimizing their operations to minimize environmental impact and to improve social outcomes in a manner that also maximizes performance.

More than two thirds of organizations we surveyed focus on CSR as part of an integrated business strategy to create new revenue streams and control costs. As a result, they face an entirely new set of decisions. Can they reduce waste without increasing the price of products? Do they need to rethink distribution options to reduce carbon and the impact of volatile energy prices? Should they segment products and services to meet a growing number of consumer sustainability concerns? The answers to these and other questions like them involve managing an intricate new set of trade-offs.

Organizations are constantly assessing the current and future impact of their activities. They're introducing innovative processes to source, distribute, develop and produce goods and services in a sustainable manner. In taking on responsibility for waste and disposal, they are charged with re-evaluating everything from product development to partnerships.

As might be expected, progress is mixed. Challenges abound, especially in accessing the information needed to meet these new strategic objectives. Overall, organizations have intensified efforts to collect information about their operations in areas from sustainable procurement to ethical labor standards. However, many are still missing – by a wide margin – the information they need to operate as a sustainable enterprise.

Outperforming organizations proved far better at casting a wide net for information across their ecosystems.[2] They are also collecting information that is more relevant to understanding and meeting the performance challenges of operating in a sustainable manner.

What is holding other organizations back? There are some very real obstacles. As is the case with many new ventures, it can be difficult to determine what information is needed. Should organizations seeking to improve sustainability look into the tsunami of real-time, unstructured information? If they do, will they know how to turn the information into insight and action? What information should they share with or request of others? And how do they manage all of these new information needs in a cost-effective way?

Early efforts suggest that collaboration is the best approach. Instead of going it alone, leading organizations are exchanging information with customers, industry groups and non-governmental organizations (NGOs) to increase their access to a wider pool of knowledge and their ability to benchmark. They are joining with partners, suppliers and even competitors to exchange leading practices and ultimately build common standards for sustainability. Standards are a requirement for effectively implementing a CSR strategy over the long term.

By collaborating and utilizing up-to-date information and standards, today's organizations can improve sustainability, while also increasing operational efficiency and performance.

EMERGING INFORMATION NEEDS

Demands for information pertaining to an organization's social and environmental impact – whether from consumers, regulators, NGOs or conscientious investors – have risen dramatically. Given today's harsh realities of global warming, increased regulation, scarcer and costlier resources and exploding populations, attention to environmental, health and societal concerns will only intensify.

Global connectivity has raised the stakes relating to a corporation's accountability for its actions. Points of view abound – on what's harmful and what's not, as well as what constitutes good business, good practice or even good sense. With the advent of the Internet, NGO scrutiny is being matched by a new kind of viral and pervasive consumer advocacy.

> Leading organizations recognize that profit at the expense of environmental or social good is ultimately not sustainable.

At the same time, the volume and granularity of information available have grown exponentially. Real-time data streams fed by sensors, satellite images, social networks, chats, videos and other mediums have greatly increased the potential to understand what's going on anywhere in the world at anytime.

Today, determining the exact field where a tree, copper or ore is extracted is as feasible as examining employees' labor rights in a factory located in a village of a thousand on the tip of an isthmus in Vietnam. With so much information available, leading organizations are finding they can satisfy the demands of a new generation of consumers: the information omnivores.

Buyers of fish, for example, have a number of concerns beyond freshness. Is the seafood really wild, as advertised? Was it harvested legally – under guidelines for total allowable catch and without endangering other ocean species? How far was it shipped and who handled it?

All of this information can be made available with today's technology. Ocean catch can be location- and time-stamped using Global Positioning System technology that tracks the position of trawlers. The data is embedded in electronic tags and transmitted all the way to point of sale so, for example, shoppers in Norway can scan barcodes to find out when and where the fish they selected was caught and packaged.[3]

Beyond reporting

Our 2009 survey reveals that sharing relevant information to educate and inform stakeholders is a primary objective. Interestingly, using information to optimize supply chains, transport and logistics, waste management and product life-cycle is a far less prevalent goal. Given that 87 percent of business leaders surveyed say they have focused their CSR efforts to create new efficiencies, we see a missed opportunity to connect operational information with this important CSR objective.

Leading organizations, however, are reaping cost efficiencies by making that connection. Chinese shipping and logistics giant COSCO was able to analyze its carbon footprint and develop alternative logistics strategies to reduce it. The company calculated trade-offs between carbon prices and consumption, logistics costs, carrier types and load capacity, information on product demand, customer service and the like. At the same time, it looked at alternative modes of transport, freight consolidation and network configuration strategies. As a result, it reduced the number of its distribution points from 100 to 40, lowering costs by 23 percent and reducing carbon dioxide emissions by 15 percent, which equates to 100,000 tons per year.[4]

Friesland Coberco Dairy Foods has taken another approach to reduce its transport burden by transforming the way it makes baby food. Ingredients that constitute the flavor varieties are now added at a later stage in the supply chain, a change that can cut inventory and transportation by an estimated 127,000 miles per year, with corresponding carbon reductions.[5]

> It's important not only to collect operational information but to do it frequently – so that fresh, accurate data can be used to make operations more sustainable.

IBM is another example. At one of its sites, it analyzes real-time data on water usage and quality collected by hundreds of sensors across the plant. Results of process improvements based on this information have already reduced overall water usage by 27 percent while increasing manufacturing production by more than 30 percent. Savings so far have amounted to $US3 million a year.

The cost efficiencies that can be gained from better management in areas such as water, energy and waste are apparent and achievable. However, there are some burdens associated with acquiring and managing a rich set of information about operations. For example, implementing sustainability strategies requires a sound understanding of trade-offs related to areas such as quality and customer service, as well as costs and environmental impact. In many cases, these factors must be evaluated for their impact across the full supply chain and life-cycle, and that requires information on how the product or service is consumed.

Food company Truitt Bros Inc. worked with the Institute for Environmental Research and Education for a full "cradle-to-plate" evaluation of the environmental impact of its single-serving shelf-stable chili and beans product. It analyzed scientific data related to climate change, soil loss and ecotoxicity caused by energy usage in food transport and manufacturing, as well as materials used in production and disposal. The investigators came to the counterintuitive conclusion that the prepared product was, overall, more environmentally friendly than a home-made bowl of chili. The finished product doesn't require freezing or refrigeration during distribution or home storage and creates less food waste. These extended supply chain factors offset the energy consumed in the manufacturing of product packaging.[6]

In addition to information about its own operations, an organization should seek full ecosystem information about its partners. A company's carbon footprint, for example, is the sum total of all footprints associated with those who supply its resources, as well as those who distribute its products. Further, when it comes to CSR, customers are among the most important partners. So, in addition to knowing how they use and dispose of products, a company needs to understand its customers' specific sustainability concerns to meet their objectives or educate customers about why the company thinks its objectives should also be theirs.

THE OPTIMIZATION GAP

We surveyed leaders on three information areas related to sustainability: operations, supply chain and customers. Our results indicate that operational information needs to be more timely, that supply chain information is still too insular and that more customer information is needed.

FIGURE 2 **CHANGE IN INFORMATION COLLECTION OVER THE PAST THREE YEARS** *(Percent responses)*

Source: IBM Institute for Business Value 2009 CSR Study.

Operational information: Growing, but not always timely

Four in ten of the business leaders surveyed reported that over the past three years they have increased the amount of information they collect about their operations in each of eight sustainability areas we tracked: energy management, carbon management, waste management, water management, sustainable procurement, product composition, ethical labor standards and product life-cycle. Not surprisingly, the biggest increase in the amount of information collected is in energy, where slightly less than two thirds of respondents report increases (see Figure 2). About half report increases in carbon, water and waste management; sustainable procurement; product composition; and ethical labor standards.

One of the great advantages of the new information era is the availability of real-time data. Yet, too often the information being collected is stale. Nearly 60 percent of organizations are not collecting information about key operations and sustainability objectives on a frequent basis. Even in the high-profile area of carbon management, for example, eight out of ten business leaders surveyed are not. They may be able to use the information they have for an annual CSR report; however, since they aren't evaluating the ongoing impact of actions on their carbon footprint, it's unlikely they can use the data to make their operations more sustainable (see Figure 3).

FIGURE 3 **FREQUENCY OF INFORMATION COLLECTION** *(Percent responses)*

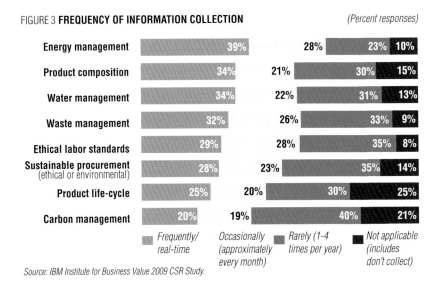

Source: IBM Institute for Business Value 2009 CSR Study.

Outperforming organizations in our survey were significantly more likely to collect timely information about their operations. For all companies, peer pressure and persistence may drive those numbers up. The longer a company has been required by its business partners to adopt CSR standards, the more frequently it collects data. This association holds true across each of the eight areas we tracked, suggesting that over time the value of truly current information becomes apparent.

Supply chain information: Still too insular

More than half of the business leaders surveyed said they consider the open sharing of information among stakeholders and business partners a high priority. However, the vast majority aren't collecting adequate information from their suppliers to support their CSR objectives. Outperforming organizations, on the other hand, are collecting more information from their suppliers in each of the eight categories we tracked as compared with their peers.

Three out of ten organizations surveyed aren't asking their suppliers for any information in any of the eight categories. Surprisingly, in the carbon and water categories, where cross-ecosystem "footprinting" is becoming more common, about eight out of ten aren't collecting information from their suppliers. And, despite a long history of brand-damaging scandals in the area of labor, six out of ten aren't collecting information on ethical labor practices from their suppliers (see Figure 4).

FIGURE 4 **INFORMATION COLLECTION FROM SUPPLIERS** *(Percent responses)*

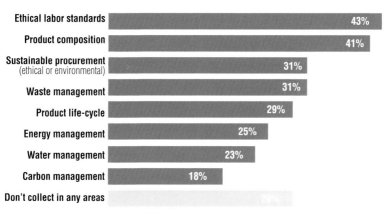

Source: IBM Institute for Business Value 2009 CSR Study.

Customer information: Improving but a long way to go

Consumer purchasing decisions are often influenced by perceptions of how socially and environmentally responsible an organization is. To see how well those perceptions are understood, we asked business leaders in our 2008 and 2009 surveys how well they understand their customers' CSR concerns. Overall in 2009, two thirds admitted they don't understand their customers' CSR concerns well. This represents an 11-point improvement over the previous year and suggests organizations are making inroads fast. Nevertheless, in our 2009 survey, nearly four in ten organizations

FIGURE 5 **YEARS CONDUCTING RESEARCH ON CUSTOMERS' CSR CONCERNS** *(Percent responses)*

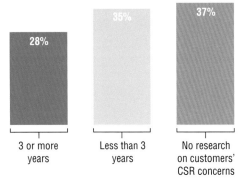

28%   35%   37%

| 3 or more years | Less than 3 years | No research on customers' CSR concerns |

Source: IBM Institute for Business Value 2009 CSR Study.

Most organizations surveyed need to collect more CSR data from suppliers, as well as gain a better understanding of their customers' CSR concerns.

reported that they have yet to conduct any research on the topic (see Figure 5). Outperforming organizations were almost twice as likely to understand their customers' needs well.

Knowledge of customers' CSR concerns varied widely by region. Nearly half of Western European business leaders say that their companies understand their customers' CSR expectations well. While that number was slightly lower in North America, it was as low as roughly one in ten in Asia Pacific. Not surprising, more than half of the companies in this region have yet to conduct any research on the topic. However, it appears companies in Asia Pacific could be moving forward. Nearly three quarters say that they have a moderate understanding of their customers' CSR expectations and nearly one fifth began researching customer concern on this topic within the past year.

Across the entire sample, the shortfall in collecting information related to operations, supply chain and customers reveals an optimization gap (see Figure 6). In addition, we found that outperforming organizations perform better in all three information categories, as do organizations that have focused for more than three years on integrating their CSR objectives to increase revenues and become more efficient. The approach to information and actions taken by these organizations suggest that the gap will narrow over time. The immediate challenge is to identify what information is needed and then aggregate and analyze it so it contributes to efficiency and growth objectives.

INSIGHT, ENGAGEMENT AND ACTION

Today, every organization is a system of systems, much more bound up in complex, interdependent forces than the traditional business system of years past, with its clear-cut focus on profits.

Given increasingly finite resources, businesses depend on balanced natural ecosystems for raw materials, water, energy and the physical health of their employees and customers. They depend on thriving community systems for labor, new sources of innovation and customers. Given the links among its systems, an enterprise committed to practicing sustainability considers both the immediate and far-reaching consequences of any action it takes.

While these dependencies obviously complicate the task of responsible business management, leaders of sustainable organizations are learning to understand and act on them. Mastering this complexity requires new levels of insight, new sources of information and new forms of collaboration. As a result, leaders in CSR are developing coalitions of business partners, NGOs and others to begin to address information gaps in areas ranging from labor to water standards. They are identifying leading practices and techniques to inform and educate stakeholders, such as customers and employees, more broadly.

Overall, most organizations know they need to engage their stakeholders in some way. However, proactive engagement with business partners and NGOs, at 55 and 44 percent respectively, is relatively low, given the benefits that can be achieved from collaboration (see Figure 7).

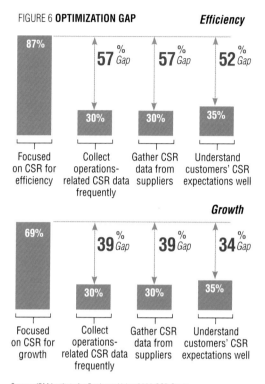

FIGURE 6 **OPTIMIZATION GAP**   *Efficiency*

Source: IBM Institute for Business Value 2009 CSR Study.

The new information landscape

The volume and granularity of information are increasing exponentially. New types of information are emerging to address challenges that were once impenetrable. Earthmine, for example, is creating a three-dimensional index of urban spaces – collecting GPS data for every pixel they capture – to help policy makers and community leaders manage public safety and economic development.[7] Another organization, Mobile Metrix, is gathering data on job skills, health conditions, education levels and more on the one billion-plus individuals in developing countries with virtually no official records.[8]

Yet another organization, Lanworth, is applying data analytics to its immense database of satellite imagery, field samples and weather models to better manage risk associated with land use and crop yields.[9] Historical information on climate, topography and production can eventually enable all stakeholders to make informed recommendations about land usage and natural resource procurement.

FIGURE 7 **PROACTIVE ENGAGEMENT WITH STAKEHOLDER GROUPS** *(Percent responses)*

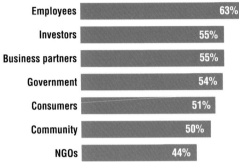

Employees 63%
Investors 55%
Business partners 55%
Government 54%
Consumers 51%
Community 50%
NGOs 44%

Source: IBM Institute for Business Value 2009 CSR Study.

New tools and services are also fast emerging to help collect information. Digitized sensors can gather and transmit information about conditions in the real world instantaneously. Pachube, for example, lets organizations freely share and monitor real-time environmental data across a global network of shared sensors.[10] Other services, such as Efficiency 2.0, combine energy audit software and social networking tools to help corporations access and act on granular data about energy usage down to the level of individual employees.[11]

Creating leading practices and standards

Today, despite a proliferation of regulations, labeling schemes and codes of conduct, standards for sustainability are relatively immature. One recent survey by the Carbon Disclosure Project revealed 34 different ways to define and measure carbon emissions among the *Financial Times* 500 companies.[12]

At present, shared leading practices and benchmarking from industry coalitions are driving CSR decision-making more so than internationally accepted standards. From these activities, however, long-lasting standards should emerge. Active industry participation today is one way to help ensure that the new practices and codes that emerge will make it easier, not more onerous, to operate a sustainable business. Moreover, industry coalitions are an excellent way to access and share a wider body of sustainability information. These groups can also help organizations make better use of their information by suggesting how, for example, the information can be deployed to change operations and innovate, as well as communicate progress to stakeholders.

Like carbon, water is a topical issue, particularly in developing countries facing scarcity of this vital resource. Well-known brands have learned the hard way that in places where government stewardship is considered inadequate, local communities will advocate in its place. To address this need, 12 companies, including Coca-Cola, Diageo, Nestlé, Anheuser-Busch InBev and PepsiCo, have formed the Beverage Industry Environmental Roundtable to collect and share data and leading practices relating to water conservation and resource protection. Together, they established a common framework to exchange information on water reduction, reuse and stewardship, as well as drought preparedness.[13]

In the electronics industry, a contract manufacturing company in Asia or Mexico would find it inefficient and effectively impossible to comply with multiple codes of conduct mandated by its original equipment manufacturer (OEM) customers. As one response to this industry challenge, the Electronics Industry Citizenship Coalition created mechanisms for companies to exchange resources and programs that improve labor practices. Audit results, along with assessment tools and educational resources, are available to association members, who span four tiers of the supply chain. Openness like this deepens relationships among OEMs, suppliers and partners, who can then harmonize their approaches to creating an ethical supply chain.

> New types of information are emerging, as are new tools and services to collect, analyze and utilize data.

Benchmarks and leading practices are important guides to use in setting objectives. The challenge lies in aligning these objectives across constituencies with diverse concerns and goals of their own. These stakeholders include employees, consumers, business partners, investors and NGOs, as well as regulatory bodies and governmental institutions. Many trade and industry organizations are developing frameworks and scorecards to help identify metrics and key performance indicators weighted to align and achieve objectives.

Wal-Mart Stores Inc. established the Packaging Sustainable Value Network, a group of 200 leaders in the packaging industry, to create a packaging scorecard with nine specific metrics that enabled suppliers to compare packaging materials, energy efficiencies, environmental standards and more against their competitors.[14] The weighted metrics give suppliers the chance to focus on specific innovations with the most impact, as well as drive constant change.

Customers: Partners in sustainability

Most organizations understand expectations for transparency with regard to CSR initiatives. More than half of the business leaders we surveyed consider the open sharing of information a high priority. However, until recently, organizations have tended to share information reactively – in response to stakeholder demands. Those that expect to gain business advantage from CSR are developing new ways to inform and educate their stakeholders, whether they are customers, employees or partners.

Many organizations are reconfiguring transport and logistics operations and weighing the trade-offs. For example, customer satisfaction may increase with conveniences such as one-day delivery, but fully loaded transport reduces energy costs. One way to evaluate the options: make the customer part of the decision. This could include laying out the shipping alternatives for customers when they make their purchases. Point-of-sale information on delivery options could provide them with a welcome opportunity to reduce their carbon footprint: "If you want to reduce your greenhouse gas emissions by 80 percent on the delivery of this television, click here and your package will arrive next week via hybrid carrier."

UK retailer Tesco makes education a mutual endeavor. Its new pilot program enables customers to recycle when they buy. Before taking purchases home, customers can take off product packaging they don't need and leave it in the supermarket. That way, they do their recycling when it is top of mind and convenient but, just as important, their actions give the retailer helpful information regarding which components of the packaging are useful enough to keep and which are excessive.[15]

German wholesaler Metro Cash & Carry created a two-way information exchange based on consumers' desire for product information. Star Farm, its wholly owned subsidiary, developed a program explaining its food traceability system and how to use in-store terminal tracking machines to scan traceability barcodes for information. Suppliers that co-operate with Star Farm and sell products have been audited and instructed by Star Farm using international quality standards. An after-sales service also allows consumers to log into Star Farm's website from home and search for product information by traceability code. In the process of answering customers' questions, these electronic searches also capture shoppers' queries, thereby deepening Metro's understanding of customer concerns about food safety and quality.

Innovations such as these help create a business culture that makes two-way transparency core to sustainability. Results from our survey indicate that organizations placing a higher priority on transparency and those that have attained some maturity find it easier to execute. Clearly, once organizations start efforts to increase transparency, they gain needed experience and greater confidence in the value of sharing information both within their organization and with their stakeholders. Engineered creatively, these collaborations can do more than inform customers. Instead of simply sharing information, organizations are learning to construct a true exchange, where both the stakeholder and the organization gain knowledge to do something new.

CONCLUSION

Organizations that seek to adopt a sustainable approach to business face a new set of decisions imposed by the constraints of finite resources. At the same time, there is a growing body of information ready to be turned into new intelligence and new advantage.

To succeed, your organization should consider the following actions:

- **Identify information gaps and analysis needs.** Is the CSR information you collect relevant and timely enough to make strategic decisions? Are you getting the information you need from your business partners and suppliers? Do you understand your customers' CSR concerns as well as those of other key stakeholders in your ecosystem?
- **Align objectives with those of stakeholders, then prioritize.** Stakeholders require a lot of information, but their information demands can't be your only focus. Are you collecting information that helps you meet your business objectives and are you communicating those objectives to all of the stakeholders?

- **Assess leading practices and benchmarks**. Have you identified sustainability leading practices and benchmarks for your key CSR activities? Are you participating in industry- or activity-focused coalitions that are developing leading practices and benchmarks? Are there frameworks or scorecards to weigh the impact of activities against overall objectives?

The answers to these questions can help you set and prioritize a course of action. As these actions advance your CSR strategy, you'll be well positioned to reap the business benefits of more efficient operations and better balance with diverse social and environmental ecosystems.

ABOUT THE AUTHORS

Eric Riddleberger is a Partner with IBM Global Business Services and leads the Global Business Strategy practice, as well as the Strategy and Transformation practice in the communications sector. He has more than 25 years of experience in strategy and technology throughout the world with IBM, Booz Allen Hamilton, UBS Capital and AT&T. His work with clients includes corporate transformation, market analysis, strategic planning, mergers and acquisitions and business development. He can be reached at eriddle@us.ibm.com.

Jeffrey Hittner is the CSR leader for IBM Global Business Services. He works with a range of industries and clients to address the emerging role of CSR and sustainability in core business strategies. His previous IBM publications include "Mastering Carbon Management" and "Attaining Sustainable Growth Through Corporate Social Responsibility." He can be reached at jhittner@us.ibm.com.

REFERENCES

1   The IBM Institute for Business Value in co-operation with the Economist Intelligence Unit surveyed senior executives across Europe, the Americas and Asia Pacific from December 2008 through January 2009.

2   Respondents classified themselves as outperforming, on par or underperforming as compared with their peers.

3   "Tracing the Fish." Seafood from Norway. March 24, 2006. http://www. seafoodfromnorway.com/page?id=100&key=14373

4   "Oh, The Climate Outside Is Frightening ..." IBM Press Release. January 23, 2009. http://www-03.ibm.com/press/us/en/pressrelease/26522.wss

5   "Mastering Carbon Management." IBM Institute for Business Value. 2008.

6   "Oregon Food Processor First to Use a Life-Cycle Assessment to Evaluate Environmental Impact of Producing and Packaging a Food Product." CSRwire. May 12, 2009. http://www.csrwire.com/press/press_release/14170-Oregon-Food-Processor-First-to-Use-a-Life-Cycle-Assessment-to-Evaluate-the-Environmental-Impact-of-Producing-and-Packaging-a-Food-Product

7   "Earthmine applications." Earthmine. http://www.earthmine.com

8   Mobile Metrix website. http://www.mobilemetrix.org

9   Lanworth website. http://lanworth.com

10 Pachube website. http://www.pachube.com

11 "Efficiency2.0: About." Efficiency2.0. http://efficiency20.com/about.html; "Efficiency2.0: Companies." Efficiency2.0. http://efficiency20.com/companies.html; "Efficiency2.0: Personal Energy Advisor." Efficiency2.0. http://efficiency20.com/software/energy_advisor.html

12 "Report Analyzes Greenhouse Gas Reporting Methods." Greenbiz.com. July 6, 2008. http://www.greenbiz.com/news/2008/07/07/greenhouse-gas-reporting-methods

13 "Water: A Global Innovation Outlook Report." IBM. 2009.

14 "Wal-Mart Unveils 'Packaging Scorecard' to Suppliers." Wal-Mart Stores, Inc. http://walmartstores.com/FactsNews/NewsRoom/6039.aspx

15 "Tesco Seeks Customers' Help in Identifying Excessive Packaging." Triplepundit. com. April 7, 2009. http://www.triplepundit.com/pages/tesco-seeks-customers-help-in-identifyin.php

Insights Leading a sustainable enterprise

More than 1,000 CEOs engaged with IBM in the discussions that underpin *The Enterprise of the Future*. In a series of follow-up video interviews conducted for the study by 50 Lessons, the world's premier multimedia business resource – and in interviews previously conducted by 50 Lessons – some of the world's top business leaders speak to the study's key themes.

Neville Isdell, the former Chairman and CEO of The Coca-Cola Company, on working with local communities.

As you look at globalization, you have to look at it in two ways, because the requirements of the era that got the likes of Coca-Cola to being, almost, a global company are different from the requirements for a globalizing company to be successful in the future. In the past it was about putting out your footprint, alone. Now I think it's a little more than that.

The way that I like to look at it is this: In this world today, where globalization is being queried, where there is potential for the rise of economic nationalism, you have to be an integral and functioning part, both in perception and in reality, of every community in which you operate. The franchise system's great, because it enables you to do that, because by and large you are working with local companies and local entrepreneurs. You are localized.

That connection back to the culture of each of those societies, in the right way, is what one has to achieve to be a successfully globalizing company. The days of parachuting in and thinking that you bring superior knowledge and expertise into some of these countries is not necessarily true. You have to identify yourselves with the societies as a whole.

One of the areas that we have identified, and which is very important to us, is water. Water is, obviously, integral to what we do. Now, how do people view our access to water? In some instances, where we haven't had what you might want to call social license, it's seen that when we are taking the water, extracting it and not adding anything back, that maybe our legitimacy can be queried. I don't believe that is a correct interpretation, but that is a reality, and I say it in terms of the perception that some people have. So what do you do?

> "That connection back to the culture of each of those societies, in the right way, is what one has to achieve to be a successfully globalizing company."

There are areas in Kenya, for example, that are water-stressed. Do we have a major issue in Kenya? No. We have a major program providing water to schools, and we do this with NGOs. We're also in certain water-stressed areas, looking after the watershed, to see that the aquifer is properly replenished.

And, of course, we're also reducing our own footprint, our own usage of water, in terms of being sure that we're able to be as effective and efficient as possible. And while it doesn't always work perfectly, that really is what you have to do.

I've taken a specific example that is relevant to Coca-Cola. You need – always – to focus on something that is relevant to your business. Otherwise, you won't take it seriously, you won't do it well and your people will not identify with it.

E. Neville Isdell was Chairman and CEO of The Coca-Cola Company from 2004 till 2008. The Coca-Cola Company, the world's top soft drink company, makes or licenses more than 400 drink products in more than 200 countries.

Anders Dahlvig, former Group President and CEO of IKEA, on promoting a social and environmental agenda.
In the past we had crises related to social and environmental issues. In the 1990s we were accused of child labor violations at suppliers in our factories in Pakistan, for example. And in the mid-1990s we received negative publicity in Germany over formaldehyde in our furniture. Our response to that was fairly reactive and defensive, and it showed us that we did not have a comprehensive agenda for CSR within the company. One of my first objectives at IKEA was to build a strong foundation, a strong agenda in terms of environmental and social issues.

Our retail people were very much in favor of a strong agenda that placed demands on our suppliers, whereas people at the supply end were fearful that purchase prices would go up. There were many debates about whether we should be at the forefront of this and be the good example, whether we should be mainstream or simply meet the minimum required by the law. It was not easy to reach agreement on how we would like to position the brand.

"You could call it a moral issue, of course, but if you want to be successful with it in your business environment, you have to have a business connection."

We took a year to discuss this broadly in the organization – at the board level, in retail, in purchasing. In retrospect it was a good idea to take that time, because this is not a subject like any other. It's an emotional subject, and it goes very deep. It's about morals and ethics; it's not just a business issue. After this long internal debate, we managed to agree that IKEA should set a good example and be at the forefront. We decided this would be beneficial for IKEA in terms of its business.

The focus areas in the beginning were those areas where we had been criticized. So we moved strongly in the area of the demands on the supplier base. Also, wood is a big part of our business and we needed to get control of the source and how it was being used at our suppliers. The third area was to create healthy and safe products, which is, of course, at the core of any business.

Today IKEA has a very good reputation when it comes to social and environmental issues. It was important 10 years ago, but it's even more important today. These issues have grown enormously in importance in society at large.

You could call it a moral issue, of course, but if you want to be successful with it in your business environment, you have to have a business connection. People have to see that this makes sense from a purely financial point of view. You can't just drive it with the moral aspect.

And it's interesting to see that it actually does help the bottom line, not only in terms of reputation but also in terms of cost reduction. At the end of the day, what's good for the environment is very often using less raw materials and resources, and less resources means lower costs. So I think there is a very good fit between the business case and the environmental agenda.

"And it's interesting to see that it actually does help the bottom line, not only in terms of reputation but also in terms of cost reduction."

Anders Dahlvig was the Group President and CEO of IKEA, a leading international retailer of home furnishing products, for 10 years until September 2009. IKEA offers more than 12,000 products and has 300 stores in 37 countries. From 1998 to 2008, sales grew from 6.3 billion euros to more than 21.2 billion euros.

These insights are drawn from interviews published by Harvard Business Press in Built for Change, *an exclusive edition of the Lessons Learned series and the result of a content partnership between IBM and 50 Lessons.*

Continuing the discussion
The 2010 Global CEO Study

One of the key findings of *The Enterprise of the Future* was that successful organizations do not fear change. Instead, they embrace it. What is now clear is that the global financial crisis of 2008-09 and its longer-term effects will truly test their capabilities.

We believe fundamental shifts are occurring as part of the new economic environment. Sweeping global economic change has ushered in a new level of uncertainty – the boundaries between the public and private spheres and the balance between global and local are shifting; competition for scarce resources is heating up; and the volume of information to be processed is increasing exponentially. In other words, the global economy will not simply return to "normal."

And so, as part of our continuing efforts to rethink the enterprise, the 2010 Global CEO Study will explore the new environment within which organizations operate, how enterprises will create advantage and what longer-term actions will enable successful leadership in the future.

The 2010 CEO Study will first examine the characteristics and requirements of the new economic environment. Then it will determine what new business models are most likely to succeed in the context of increased complexity and uncertainty. The study will look at new ways in which companies can take advantage of increased connectivity and harness the value of information. It will identify the personal leadership characteristics, qualifications and behaviors that best suit the new environment. And it will discuss how organizations can create compelling plans to deliver real results – and do so in short order so as to maximize competitive gains.

In short, we view *Rethinking the Enterprise* not as an end, but rather as a catalyst for future discussions about where business and enterprises are headed. We look forward to working with you to build your Enterprise of the Future.

Saul Berman, Peter Korsten and Ragna Bell

Continue the conversation: www.ibm.com/gbs/ceostudy

IBM Global Business Services

With business experts in more than 170 countries, IBM Global Business Services provides clients with deep business process and industry expertise across 17 industries, using innovation to identify, create and deliver value faster. We draw on the full breadth of IBM capabilities, standing behind our advice to help clients implement solutions designed to deliver business outcomes with far-reaching impact and sustainable results.

IBM Global Business Services Strategy and Change Practice

IBM Global Business Services offers one of the largest Strategy and Change consulting practices in the world, with more than 3,000 strategy professionals. Our Strategy and Change practice fuses business strategy with technology insight to help organizations develop, align and implement their business vision across four strategic dimensions – business strategy, operating strategy, organization change strategy and technology strategy – to drive innovation and growth.

IBM Institute for Business Value

The IBM Institute for Business Value, part of IBM Global Business Services, develops fact-based strategic insights for senior business executives around critical industry-specific and cross-industry issues.